The Creative Hostess
EDINBURGH
COOKBOOK

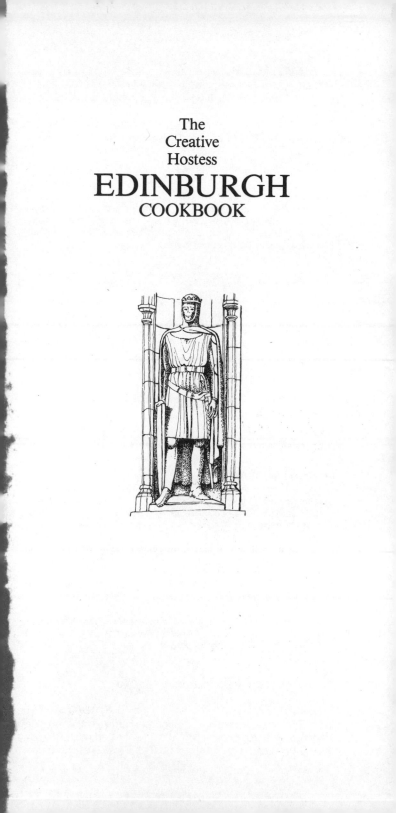

We would like to thank all those who have helped us in the preparation of this book, and all the restaurateurs and chefs listed on pages 78-9 who have so kindly provided us with recipes.

Editor: Melanie Bradman   Researcher: Isabel Papadakis

THE CITY EMBLEM

Depicting things of importance in Edinburgh's history, the emblem shows the castle and a stag from which King David I miraculously escaped (see page 22). The city motto 'Nisi Dominus Frustra' reminds us that you cannot do much without God's help!

ROBERT THE BRUCE *(previous page)*

Spot Scotland's famous king in the Castle Gatehouse.

THE SCOTT MONUMENT *(opposite)*

With its spires and pinnacles, this splendid Gothic memorial to the romantic novelist, Sir Walter Scott, soars 200 feet above Princes Street. Its intricate detail includes representations of famous Scottish poets and heroes, plus 64 characters from Scott's novels.

To help them reach a decision as to what would canopy Sir John Steele's statue of Scott and his dog Maida, the Edinburgh authorities launched a competition. The winner, Kemp, was relatively unknown and there was considerable resentment amongst more famous competitors. The monument was inaugurated in 1844.

From the uppermost of four galleries built above the monument's principal arches, there are breathtaking views of the City. It is a climb of 287 steps, but well worth the effort!

First published March 1984 by   ISBN 0 904330 69 9
Marion Edwards Limited,   Second Impression, June 1984
69 Abingdon Road,   Printed in England by
Kensington, London W8 6AW   T.J. Press (Padstow) Ltd.

The
Creative Hostess
EDINBURGH
COOKBOOK

WITH DRAWINGS OF THE CITY BY
HELEN FOX

Introduction

Surprising as it may sound, the cooks and camp followers of Robert the Bruce's army are supposed to have been largely responsible for the Scottish victory over the English at the Battle of Bannockburn in 1314 — a date firmly imprinted on the minds of all Scottish schoolchildren.

Apparently the cooks appeared on the brow of a hill waving their ladles and chopping knives in such a war-like fashion that the English, thinking they were another wing of the Scottish army, turned tail and retreated in horror!

Today the opposite may be said to be the case, with the restaurants and hotels of Edinburgh playing host to visitors from all over the world (and even making the English welcome!). The fare they offer ranges from traditional Scottish to Oriental, but their welcome is always as warm as their whisky. Within these pages are recipes from some of their best chefs — and we didn't have to threaten any of them with a chopping knife (or even a ladle) to get them to reveal their secrets!

Whether you use this little volume to help you discover the culinary delights and historical curios the City has to offer, or if you simply want a small memento to enjoy at your leisure, we feel sure you will find within its pages recipes to enjoy and memories to treasure of present day Scottish hospitality and echoes from the past. Talking of which, if you think you hear the echo of marching feet on Castle Esplanade, don't be surprised — ghostly batallions have been seen and heard there since 1650.

A note on measures and conversions
Ingredients are given in metric, Imperial and American measures. **Use measures from one column only.** Teaspoon and tablespoon measures in the metric column correspond to 5 ml and 15 ml respectively. Unless otherwise stated, all fruits and vegetables used should be medium sized.

THE NATIONAL MONUMENT

Built in memory of Scots killed in the Napoleonic wars, this replica of the Parthenon in Athens is something of an embarrassment, since it was never finished due to lack of funds — the money ran out half way through construction!

Contents

Recipes

Historical Notes

The City of Edinburgh

The City's origins

Edinburgh's ancient name was 'Dunedin', which means fortress on a sloping ridge. Unique among capital cities because of its extraordinary location — it was neither built beside a major river, nor did it grow up on a plain — the settlement straggled along a precarious, rocky ridge. The only approach to the fortified castle, first established by the Picts as long ago as A.D. 452, this ridge was the product of volcanic heat and a slow moving glacier millions of years ago.

The City derives its present-day name from its status as a royal *burgh* conferred on it in the fourteenth century by Robert the Bruce, and possibly from the Northumbrian King *Edwin* who re-built the castle in the seventh century.

Turbulent times

Scotland's history sometimes looks like chapter upon chapter of invasions and foreign occupations. Nevertheless, while it is easy to gain the impression that the Scots were constantly pitched against unfriendly outsiders such as the Roman invaders in A.D. 78 or the English redcoats in the 18th century they were also, as often as not, fighting amongst themselves! The Picts were quarrelsome tribes and the Gaelic monarchs themselves left a bloody trail behind them. Take, for example, the gruesome murder of the young Earl of Douglas and his brother, slain after they had dined in the banqueting hall. Then there is the story which Shakespeare used for his 'Macbeth'. Duncan really was a Scottish king who was killed by Macbeth. In fact it was Duncan's son Malcolm (also in the play) who was the last purely Gaelic king. He married the anglo-saxon Margaret and they had six sons, three of them becoming kings!

THE ROYAL SCOTTISH ACADEMY FROM HANOVER STREET

With the Old Town rising behind it in layers of architectural variety, William Playfair's Royal Academy, built in 1823, spreads out at the bottom of the Mound like a splendid classical temple. The uniform base gives way to magnificent fluted columns and eight sphinxes grace the roof. However, in the midst of such classicism, is a statue of Queen Victoria! Despite the patriotic intention, Her Majesty looks somewhat ill at ease in her classical robes!

Amid these bloody feuds, both internal and external, Edinburgh early emerged as a political, military and cultural stronghold and has been acknowledged as Scotland's capital for over 500 years.

The medieval town

Where the Picts built their fortified castle a settlement inevitably began to grow, but construction was considerably limited because of the nature of the terrain.

Other factors also influenced the town's unusual, linear growth. First, in the 15th century, building was restricted by royal decree from developing upwards towards the summit of the rock and so from encroaching the castle's territory. A wall was actually built to separate the city from the castle. Perhaps James II, the monarch responsible, was bothered by the city's smells since it was a notoriously dirty place!

In 1513, the English beat the Scots severely at the Battle of Flodden. The inhabitants of Edinburgh were so frightened of further English attacks that they built the 'Flodden Wall' to protect themselves. This defence shaped Edinburgh's development for the next 250 years since it was not until after the 'Act of Union' between England and Scotland that the people of Edinburgh felt safe enough to build their homes beyond the wall.

Canongate

The Burgh of Canongate is now almost indistinguishable from the Royal Burgh of Edinburgh, the Netherbow port which stood between Canongate and the High Street having been demolished. Once the two areas were distinct and separate.

Continued on page 10

10

Continued from page 7

Canongate had associations with Holyrood Abbey, the name Canongate deriving from the Canons of the Abbey who were first given permission to build in the area beyond the Abbey walls. However, unlike Edinburgh, Canongate had no protective wall and was vulnerable to invasions from the south.

The Royal Mile

The medieval city lies between the Castle and Holyrood-house, and the road joining them is known as the Royal Mile, running for approximately that distance along the ridge between the two royal residences: the Castle and Holyrood-house, palace of the Stuart dynasty and of our reigning monarch, Queen Elizabeth II.

The Queen is Sovereign of the Order of the Thistle, the oldest and most prestigious Scottish order of chivalry, created by James III in the fifteenth century. There are at present sixteen Knights of the Thistle plus two royal holders of the Order, the Prince of Wales and the Duke of Edinburgh, a Lady of the Thistle (The Queen Mother), and an additional knight, the King of Norway. The Thistle Chapel in St Giles' Kirk was consecrated in 1911, and it is there, on the Order's ceremonial occasions, that the knights are to be seen in the magnificent dark blue robes and large, feathered hats which mark their status.

The New Town

Although freed from the threat of invasion with the 'Act of Union', the inhabitants nonetheless took a long time and a lot of persuasion to actually move beyond the Flodden Wall. However, there was so much overcrowding in the tall tenements (building had had to develop upwards instead of outwards!), not to speak of the terrible poverty and squalor, that the authorities were determined to make the City expand and take advantage of the increasing trade coming up the Forth to the port of Leith.

So, in 1763 the Nor' Loch was drained and a competition organised for the development of the area north of the Old Town. A young architect called James Craig won, and the New Town of elegant squares and broad thoroughfares was born. Even so, private building had to be 'encouraged', with a £20 award to the first person to build his house in the new town!

THE MOUND When the New Town was laid out, earth from the new buildings' foundations and the drained Nor' Loch was literally piled up in a mound. It lies between east and west Princes Street Gardens, and its steep road was always a hazard in winter. Underground heating has now been installed to keep it free from ice in winter.

(Footnote!)

EDINBURGH CASTLE *(see page 8)*

During its long and turbulent history, Edinburgh Castle has been at the heart of many violent power struggles. Control of the castle, perched high on castle rock, was vital to any attacker. It is almost impregnable, being 443 feet above sea level and only approachable from one side, and because of its strong strategic position it was fought for bitterly, exchanging hands often.

Although records reveal that there was a tribal stronghold here as early as 600 A.D., the first reliable records date from the 11th century when Malcolm and Margaret built their fortified residence here. However, by the 12th century the castle had passed into the hands of the English. After winning it back for the Scots, Robert the Bruce devastated the early castle so that the English could never again use the site to dominate the area. However, he spared the tiny chapel believed to have been built by Queen Margaret. 900 years later, it is still standing.

The castle which today dominates the city's skyline dates from the 14th century. In its time it has been beseiged and attacked from all sides; it has served as a prison, a fortress, an arsenal and an armoury as well as a royal residence and is still as forbidding and impressive as ever. However, in complete contrast to the castle's strength, don't miss the tiny bedroom where Mary Queen of Scots gave birth to the son who was later to become James I of England and VI of Scotland, nor the tiny pets' cemetery where soldiers' dogs may be buried.

Just as the names of some of the Old Town's streets (such as Cowgate, Grass Market and Candlemakers' Row) reflect the trade and agriculture vital to the inhabitants, so the New Town's street names tell us something about Georgian society, reflecting the desire for harmony and parliamentary unity between England and Scotland.

Princes , Queen's and George Streets do homage to the royal family of the day, the latter linking two magnificent squares originally to be called St Andrew's and St George's after the patron saints of the two countries. Sadly, Queen Charlotte had other ideas, so St George had to take a bow!

The New Town also set out to display social harmony. Thistle and Rose Streets, which run between the grand boulevards, are more modest and designed to house trade and commerce.

Eighteenth century Edinburgh was an elegant city and an internationally known cultural centre. Many prominent figures of the day were Edinburgh men and, without a doubt, 'society' came to the City to walk in the new and elegant gardens, to be seen in Princes Street and to meet with the authors, poets, composers and great thinkers of the day who were attracted to Edinburgh, and who graced it with their patronage. The present day success of the Edinburgh Festival bears witness to the lasting and compelling attractions of this inspiring and beautiful capital city.

Super Starters

PARTAN BREE

Serves 4

A rich version of a traditional Scottish creamy crab soup from Chef Ronnie Reglinski of the King James Hotel.

Metric		lb/oz	U.S.A.
	½ Boiled crab		
30 g	Butter	1 oz	2 tbsp
½	Shallot, chopped	½	½
1	Nutmeg or mace, pinch of	1	1
1	Thyme, pinch of	1	1
1	Bay leaf	1	1
60 g	Plain flour	2 oz	½ cup
1 tbsp	Tomato purée	1 tbsp	1 tbsp
1 tbsp	Single cream	1 tbsp	1 tbsp
1 tbsp	Brandy	1 tbsp	1 tbsp

1. Remove the dark and white meat from the crab, keeping them separate. To make the stock, pound the shell and bones in a mortar, then bring to the boil in 900 ml (1½ pt, 3½ cups) of water. Simmer for 30 minutes then strain.
2. Melt the butter and add the shallot, spice and herbs. Season and cook gently for a few minutes.
3. Stir in the flour and cook for a further few minutes then stir in the tomato purée.
4. Strain the stock and reserve 5 tbsp. Add the rest, a little at a time, stirring continuously. Bring to the boil and simmer for 15-20 minutes.
5. Liquidize the dark crab meat and add to the stock. Bring back to the boil, re-strain, and thin with stock if necessary.
6. Just before serving, stir in the cream and brandy. Flake the white meat and use this as a garnish.

"Soup of the evening, beautiful Soup!" Alice in Wonderland
LEWIS CARROLL, 1832-1898

INKY-PINKY, BUBBLYJOCK AND BAWD BREE. If you were offered these Scottish dishes, would you know what to expect? Some are quite unintelligible to most of us. So don't forget the Inky-pinky is beef and carrot stew and Bubblyjock is roast turkey. If you are offered Bawd Bree, only accept if you like hare soup, but if you are lucky you may experience Melting Moments — in Scotland that's biscuits dipped in rolled oats. So now you know!

COCK-A-LEEKIE SOUP   *Serves 10-12*

Aptly named, this chicken and leek soup is popular with Scots and Sassenachs alike! This recipe comes from the Rutland Hotel and is served in their Le Jardin restaurant.

Metric		lb/oz	U.S.A.
	1 × 1½ kg (3 lb) Chicken		
575 g	Leeks	1¼ lb	1¼ lb
1	Bay leaf	1	1
1	Thyme, sprig of	1	1
3	Parsley stalks	3	3
2	Onions, finely chopped	2	2
60 g	Long grain rice	2 oz	⅓ cup
	Parsley, chopped		

1. Remove the roots and green tops of the leeks, then chop the white parts finely.
2. Place the chicken in a large pan and cover with 3 litres (5 pt, 12 cups) of water. Bring to the boil, then skim off the surface.
3. Tie the herbs together in a bunch and add to the pan with the chopped leek and onion. Season to taste with salt and freshly ground black pepper.
4. Cover the pan and simmer for 1½-2 hours or until the meat is tender.
5. Add the rice half an hour before the end of cooking time.
6. When cooked, remove the fowl and leave to cool. When cold enough, remove the meat and chop up roughly. Return to the soup and heat through.
7. Check the seasoning, remove the herbs and serve immediately garnished with chopped parsley.

BAKEHOUSE CLOSE, Old Fishmarket Close and Sugarhouse Close are just three of the street names in the Old Town which reveal the traders who lived there in the middle ages. Then there are Horse Wynd, Bull's Close and Cowgate (so called because it was a country lane along which cattle were driven to pasture). In Candlemakers' Row, the craft flourished from 1488 till gas lighting emerged in the 19th century.

SCOTCH BROTH   *Serves 6*

All the ingredients of this soup are traditional Scottish fare —
though most Scots would, of course, call turnips 'neeps'. This
version is served at the Ellersly House Hotel and the recipe was
provided by Chef Hogg.

Metric		lb/oz	U.S.A.
30 g	Barley	1 oz	¼ cup
30 g	Dried peas	1 oz	¼ cup
2	Carrots	2	2
2	Onions	2	2
2	Turnips	2	2
2	Leeks	2	2
60 g	Butter	2 oz	¼ cup
1.25 litres	Lamb stock	2 pt	5 cups

1. Soak the barley and peas in cold water overnight, then
   drain and rinse.
2. Clean the vegetables and cut into ½ cm (¼") cubes.
3. Melt the butter in a large pan and sauté the vegetables.
4. Add the barley, peas and stock and bring to the boil.
   Season to taste.
5. Simmer for 1½ hours and serve immediately.

THE BURIED BOY

This charming carving above the entrance to Paisley Close
commemorates the rescuing of a brave little boy when nearby
tenements collapsed in 1861, killing 35 people. From beneath the
rubble, rescuers heard his calm, collected voice calling 'Heave awa
chaps, I'm no' dead yet!'.

MORAY PLACE

One of the grandest specimens of the New Town, this Georgian development is typical of the elegance and symmetry of the period. In 1822, Lord Moray advertised the land for development. Such was the demand for houses on so superior a site that by 1827 almost all were sold. Lord Moray himself lived at number 28.

TOWN HOUSE BOOT SCRAPER The building of the New Town did not eradicate the problem of muddy streets. These original scrapers can still be seen by front doors, but also look out for those actually built into the iron railings.

CHINESE VEGETABLE SOUP   *Serves 6*

This oriental speciality of the Cringletie House Hotel, Peebles, makes a light but tasty start to a meal.

Metric		lb/oz	U.S.A.
1.25 litres	*Chicken stock*	2 pt	5 cups
1 tbsp	*Mushrooms, sliced*	1 tbsp	1 tbsp
1 tbsp	*Bean sprouts*	1 tbsp	1 tbsp
1 tbsp	*Celery, thinly sliced*	1 tbsp	1 tbsp
1 tbsp	*Chinese leaves or lettuce, finely shredded*	1 tbsp	1 tbsp
1 tbsp	*Sherry*	1 tbsp	1 tbsp
1 tbsp	*Soya sauce*	1 tbsp	1 tbsp
3 tbsp	*Chives, chopped*	3 tbsp	¼ cup

1. Bring the stock to the boil in a large pan. Add the vegetables and boil for 5 minutes.
2. Add the sherry and soya sauce, then season to taste.
3. Serve garnished with the chives.

16

LE CAVEAU'S ONION TART

A tasty vegetarian all-in-one dish popular with visitors to Le Caveau 'Club des Vins' in Dundas Street.

Metric		lb/oz	U.S.A.
5	Onions, halved and sliced	5	5
225 g	Flour	8 oz	2 cups
125 g	Butter	4 oz	½ cup
1 tbsp	Oil	1 tbsp	1 tbsp
	For the sauce:		
25 g	Butter	¾ oz	2 tbsp
25 g	Flour	¾ oz	2 tbsp
250 ml	Milk, boiled	8 fl. oz	¾ cup
150 ml	Cream	4 fl. oz	½ cup
60 g	Red Cheddar cheese, grated	2 oz	½ cup

1. Set the oven to 200°C, 400°F, Gas Mark 6.
2. Put the flour in a bowl with a pinch of salt, and rub in the butter until the mixture resembles fine breadcrumbs.
3. Make a well in the centre and bind with enough water to make a soft dough. Cover and refrigerate until needed.
4. Roll out the pastry on a floured board and line a buttered flan tin. Line the pastry with greaseproof paper and add a handful of dried lentils to stop the pastry rising.
5. Bake blind for 15-20 minutes, remove paper and lentils, and continue cooking until golden brown.
6. Heat the oil in a pan and add the onions. Fry over a gentle heat until very soft being careful not to let them brown.
7. To make the sauce, place the butter and flour in a pan and mix well together to make a roux. Add the milk slowly, stirring all the time, and bring to the boil. Season to taste. Remove from the heat and stir in the cream.
8. Pour the sauce over the onions and mix thoroughly, then transfer the mixture to the pastry case.
9. Sprinkle with the cheese and place under a hot grill until the cheese is melted and brown.

GRASSMARKET was originally an agricultural produce market, where onions were no doubt much in evidence! Lying in a hollow at the base of the Castle Rock, it was also the place where public executions took place.

AVOCADO MARRIANE   Serves 8

A creamy delicacy popular at the Post House Hotel.

Metric		lb/oz	U.S.A.
4	Avocados	4	4
250 g	Smoked haddock, flaked	8 oz	1½ cups
250 g	Crabmeat	8 oz	1½ cups
150 ml	Double cream	¼ pt	½ cup
150 ml	Hollandaise sauce (see p.70)	¼ pt	½ cup

1. Set the oven to 180°C, 350°F, Gas Mark 4.
2. Remove the avocado stones, scoop out the flesh and retain shells. Mix the flesh, crabmeat and fish, and stir in the cream to bind. Spoon into the shells, and place in a baking dish, supported with crushed foil.
3. Warm in the oven for 4-5 minutes. Remove, coat the top of the avocados with hollandaise sauce, and place under a hot grill for a few minutes to glaze. Serve immediately.

PEARS IN BLUE CHEESE   *Serves 4*

A quick and easy creation from Joan Spiler of the Laigh Kitchen.

Metric		lb/oz	U.S.A.
4	Pears*	4	4
50 g	Blue cheese	2 oz	½ cup
50 g	Cream cheese	2 oz	½ cup
4 tbsp	Mayonnaise	4 tbsp	½ cup
	Lettuce and tomato to garnish		

1. Mash the blue cheese and cream cheese together.
2. Stir in the mayonnaise and season to taste.
3. Toss the pears in the mixture, and serve on lettuce garnished with tomato.

* If fresh, peel, core and slice and sprinkle with lemon juice; if tinned, drain well.

NELSON'S MONUMENT

Standing on Calton Hill, and appropriately enough in the form of a giant telescope, this 108 feet high monument is topped by a time ball in an open shaft. It descends at 1 pm acting as a time check for ships in the Firth of Forth.

AVOCADO WITH CHEESE AND FRESH HERBS   *Serves 6*

Herbs add both colour and flavour to this otherwise simple starter from the Cringletie House Hotel, Peebles.

Metric		*lb/oz*	*U.S.A.*
3	*Avocados*	3	3
2 tbsp	*Fresh mixed herbs, chopped*	2 tbsp	2 tbsp
	— e.g. parsley, mint and thyme		
225 g	*Cream cheese*	8 oz	1 cup
1 tbsp	*Cream or top of the milk*	1 tbsp	1 tbsp
2 tbsp	*Lemon juice*	2 tbsp	2 tbsp
6	*Parsley sprigs*	6	6

1. Blend the herbs and cheese, adding just enough cream or milk to make the mixture soft enough to pipe.
2. Remove the stones from the avocados and brush the flesh with the lemon juice to prevent discolouring.
3. Pipe the cheese in whirls into the centre of the avocados and decorate with the parsley sprigs.

SOUSED HERRINGS   *Serves 4*

"Ah, Tam! ah, Tam! thou'll get thy fairin'!
In hell they'll roast thee like a herrin'!"   Tam O'Shanter
               ROBERT BURNS, 1759-1796

Once everyday fare, herring is now almost a luxury. This recipe from the Ellersly House Hotel is well worth trying.

Metric		*lb/oz*	*U.S.A.*
4	*Boneless herring fillets*	4	4
1	*Onion, sliced into rings*	1	1
1	*Carrot, sliced*	1	1
1	*Bay leaf*	1	1
10	*Peppercorns*	10	10
150 ml	*Vinegar*	¼ pt	½ cup
	Lettuce, sliced tomatoes and lemon wedges to garnish		

1. Set the oven to 150°C, 300°F, Gas Mark 2.
2. Wash and dry the herrings then lay each fillet flat, the skin side down. Lay the onion rings on top of the fish then carefully roll up and secure with a cocktail stick.
3. Lay the rolls in a deep-sided dish, side by side.
4. Put the carrot, bay leaf and peppercorns on top of the fish, add the vinegar, and enough cold water to cover. Bake in the oven for 20 minutes.
5. Remove and cool, then refrigerate until completely cold. Remove the fish from the vegetables and serve on a bed of lettuce and tomato. Garnish with the lemon.

WILD HIGHLAND MUSSELS   *Serves 4*

An exotic combination occasionally served in the Pompadour
Restaurant at the Caledonian Hotel.

Metric		lb/oz	U.S.A.
30	Fresh mussels	30	30
1	Bicarbonate of soda, pinch of	1	1
1	Bouquet garni	1	1
	For the Wild Highland Garlic butter:		
225 g	Butter	8 oz	1 cup
3 tbsp	Onion, finely chopped	3 tbsp	¼ cup
1	Garlic clove, crushed	1	1
4	Hazelnuts, crushed	4	4
3 tbsp	Parsley, chopped	3 tbsp	¼ cup
1	Anchovy fillet, crushed	1	1
2 tbsp	Malt whisky	2 tbsp	2 tbsp

1. Wash and scrub the mussels, discarding any broken ones.
   Bring to the boil in 300 ml (½ pt, 1 cup) of water with the
   bicarbonate of soda, bouquet garni and salt and pepper.
2. Reduce the heat, cover and steam the mussels for 10
   minutes until they have opened. Remove the mussels from
   the liquid and discard any that are still closed.
3. Remove the mussels from their shells, and share between 4
   warmed ramekins. Keep warm.
4. To make the topping, place all the remaining ingredients in
   a pan and heat slowly, stirring until the butter has melted.
5. Pour the garlic butter over the mussels and serve very hot.

PICKLED LEMON KIPPERS   *Serves 8*

This unusual recipe comes from Chef William Marshall of the
Roxburghe Hotel. Note the preparation time required!

Metric		lb/oz	U.S.A.
1 kg	Kipper fillets	2 lb	2 lb
½ cup	Glycerine	½ cup	½ cup
2	Lemons, juice of	2	2
300 ml	Vinegar	½ pt	1 cup
	Black pepper		
	Lettuce and lemon wedges to garnish		

1. Cut the kippers into goujons about 3 cm (1½") long and
   place in a large shallow bowl.
2. Mix the glycerine, lemon juice and vinegar and season with
   freshly ground black pepper. Pour over the fish and
   marinate for 30 hours.
3. Remove from the marinade and drain.
4. Serve on a bed of lettuce and garnish with lemon wedges.

COCKTAIL GLENDRONACH   *Serves 4*

A Scottish version of prawn cocktail, one of the most popular
starters around, from the Caledonian Hotel in Princes Street.

Metric		lb/oz	U.S.A.
2 tbsp	Malt Scotch whisky	2 tbsp	2 tbsp
300 ml	Double cream	½ pt	1 cup
3 tbsp	Tomato ketchup	3 tbsp	¼ cup
1	Worcestershire sauce, dash of	1	1
1 tsp	Horseradish sauce	1 tsp	1 tsp
1	Lemon juice, squeeze of	1	1
4	Tomatoes, skinned and de-seeded	4	4
30 g	Onion, grated	1 oz	¼ cup
250 g	Prawns, shelled	8 oz	2 cups
	To garnish:		
4	Large, unshelled prawns	4	4
4	Spring onions	4	4
4	Orange segments	4	4
1	Tomato, quartered	1	1
4	Parsley sprigs	4	4

1. Whip the cream until stiff then stir in the tomato ketchup,
   Worcestershire sauce, horseradish sauce, lemon juice and
   half the whisky. Mix well.
2. Place the tomatoes in a pan with the onion and remaining
   whisky. Cook slowly until the moisture has evaporated.
3. Stir the tomato mixture into the sauce and divide between
   four cocktail glasses. Divide the shelled prawns between
   the glasses. Garnish each with an unshelled prawn, onion,
   orange, tomato and parsley.

CANAPE CALEDONIAN   *Serves 4*

These hot, cheese-topped croûtons from the Royal Scot Hotel
can be served as a starter, snack or end-of-the-meal savoury.

Metric		lb/oz	U.S.A.
4	Bacon rashers, chopped	4	4
4	Bread slices	4	4
	Oil for frying		
2	Tomatoes, sliced	2	2
3 tbsp	Chutney	3 tbsp	¼ cup
30 g	Butter	1 oz	2 tbsp
1 tbsp	Flour	1 tbsp	1 tbsp
75 ml	Milk	⅛ pt	⅓ cup
1	Worcestershire sauce, dash of	1	1
125 g	Cheese, grated	4 oz	1 cup
1 tsp	Curry powder	1 tsp	1 tsp

1. Cook the bacon until crispy and set aside. Using a round pastry cutter, cut two croûtons from each slice of bread and fry in the oil until lightly brown. Drain well and keep hot until required.
2. Divide the tomato, bacon and chutney between the croûtons.
3. To make the welsh rarebit, heat the butter in a pan and stir in the flour. Cook for several minutes stirring well. Stir in the milk over a gentle heat until you have a smooth, thick mixture.
4. Add the Worcestershire sauce, cheese, curry powder and a good pinch of salt and pepper.
5. Stir well and cook until the cheese has melted but do not overcook or the cheese will become oily.
6. Spoon onto the croûtons and glaze under a hot grill until brown and bubbly. Serve immediately.

COTTAGE CHEESE AND PINEAPPLE MOUSSE   *Serves 6*

Another versatile creation, this creamy mousse from the Royal Scot Hotel can also be served as a summer salad dish.

Metric		lb/oz	U.S.A.
2 tbsp	Aspic powder	2 tbsp	2 tbsp
90 g	Salted peanuts	3 oz	⅔ cup
2	Pineapple rings, diced	2	2
450 g	Cottage cheese	1 lb	2 cups
125 ml	Double cream	4 fl. oz	½ cup
½ tsp	Cayenne pepper	½ tsp	½ tsp
2 tbsp	Parsley, chopped	2 tbsp	2 tbsp

1. Dissolve the aspic in 200 ml (⅓ pt, ¾ cup) of warm water and allow to cool.
2. Arrange the peanuts in the bottom of a mould and coat with half the aspic. Put in a cool place to set.
3. Mix the pineapple with the cottage cheese and cream. Stir in the cayenne and season to taste.
4. Stir in the remaining aspic and put in a cool place until nearly set.
5. When the mixture is just setting, spoon it over the nuts and place the mould in the refrigerator to set.
6. To serve, dip the mould into hot water and turn out on to a wetted serving dish. Garnish with chopped parsley.

IF AT FIRST YOU DON'T SUCCEED ...
try, try, try again — the invaluable lesson Robert the Bruce learnt from a spider!

Royal Edinburgh

Even before becoming the official capital of Scotland when James II came to the throne in 1437, Edinburgh dominated Scottish power struggles and provided a royal residence.

David I

David was the grandson of Duncan (the king killed by Macbeth), and in 1128 he founded the ancient Holyrood Abbey. Although it later fell into disrepair the Abbey helped put Edinburgh on the map by providing the city with clerical status as well as attracting pilgrims and visitors.

Tradition has it that during a hunting outing King David was knocked from his horse by a frightened stag, but saved from further injury by the miraculous appearance of a cross between the beast's antlers. It was in gratitude for this extraordinary escape that he established the Abbey.

Robert the Bruce

Robert the Bruce granted Edinburgh the status of Royal Burgh. He is best remembered for the legendary encounter with a spider which encouraged him to persevere in his struggles against the English. He subsequently led his army to a resounding victory over the English at Bannockburn.

James IV

The reign of James IV (grandfather of Mary Queen of Scots) was one of the happiest and most colourful in Scotland's history. With his wife Margaret, sister of England's Henry VIII, James held court in the city. It was an era of renaissance and chivalry with jousting tourneys held at the king's stables in Grassmarket. Minstrels and jesters, players and musicians patronized the court, and among other things, the first Scottish printing press was established.

Edinburgh blossomed under the King's patronage and began truly to acquire the atmosphere and variety of a capital city.

Mary, Queen of Scots

The young Scottish princess who became Queen when only a few days old is one of the most romantic yet tragic of all Scottish heroines. Arriving from France as a young widow, she resided in Holyroodhouse. Her second husband Lord Darnley died in an explosion — with the Queen heavily suspected because he was widely believed to have been responsible for the murder of Mary's favourite, Rizzio.

Mary also ended her days unnaturally. Edinburgh could not tolerate her passionate Catholicism, nor her affiliation with France, and so took her Protestant son James as its monarch. England's Queen Elizabeth could not contain her Scottish cousin's rivalry for the English throne and so, after years of imprisonment, the ill-fated Mary ended her days on the block.

The fall of the House of Stuart

It was on 17th September 1745 that Bonnie Prince Charlie arrived in Edinburgh at the head of 2,000 Highlanders. He remained in the City for six weeks, during which time he held court at Holyroodhouse, even giving a ball — such was his confidence that he was going to secure the crown. Unfortunately his confidence was misplaced, and a year later the Stuarts finally had to admit defeat at Culloden.

The tartans worn by the Highlanders were originally badges of rank, finally becoming the identifying 'uniform' of particular clans. The tartan of the Royal House of Stuart sported by Bonnie Prince Charlie is now worn by our own Prince Charles and other members of the Royal Family, being the personal tartan of the monarch.

TRADITION HAS IT that the ball lodged in Cannonball House gable (near Outlook Tower in the Royal Mile) was fired at clansman during the 1745 uprising.

George IV

When George IV visited Edinburgh in 1822 it was the first official visit by a British monarch for more than two centuries, the intervening years having been troubled by opposition to the union of England and Scotland.

The George IV bridge was built to commemorate his visit. George made a big impact on the people. One day he appeared wearing a very short kilt and pink tights which prompted a lady watching to remark, 'As he is to be with us for such a short time, the more we see of him the better'!

Monarchy today

Modern associations of royalty with Edinburgh are accentuated by the title given to the British monarch's husband. Prince Philip, the Duke of Edinburgh, is Chancellor of the University, and also a Knight of the Thistle.

STATUE OF KING CHARLES II

This imposing statue by the side of the High Kirk of St Giles and depicting the King as a proud Roman emperor, barefoot and laurel crowned, was cast in lead in 1655. It is the only surviving equestrian statue of him, and on each 4th June, the King's birthday, the statue is decorated with flowers.

THE PALACE OF HOLYROODHOUSE

The official residence of the British Monarch in Scotland was begun in 1501 by James IV, but was not completed until the reign of Charles II over a hundred years later. Although its front looks like one piece of work, the twin towers were actually built over 160 years apart!

Mary Queen of Scots came to Holyrood when she arrived from France to claim her throne. Her private secretary (and suspected lover) David

Rizzio was murdered here in 1565. It was particularly gruesome as he was stabbed in her presence while she sat at supper in the James IV tower, and the spot where he fell can still be seen.

The last Stuart court to be held at Holyrood was that of the romantic but ill-fated Bonnie Prince Charlie, who gave a ball there when leading an abortive attempt to win back the throne for his father.

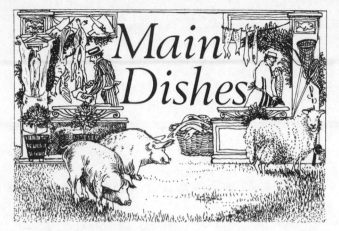

Main Dishes

SCOTCH SALMON EN CROUTE
WITH CUCUMBER SAUCE

Serves 2

Metric		lb/oz	U.S.A.
	2 x 175 g (6 oz) Scotch salmon steaks		
½	Lemon, juice of	½	½
175 g	Shortcrust pastry	6 oz	6 oz
30 g	Butter	1 oz	2 tbsp
½	Cucumber	½	½
½ tsp	Dill weed	½ tsp	½ tsp
1 tbsp	Milk to glaze	1 tbsp	1 tbsp
	For the sauce:		
150 ml	Sour cream	¼ pt	½ cup
1 tsp	Parsley, finely chopped	1 tsp	1 tsp
1 tsp	Onion, finely grated	1 tsp	1 tsp

1. Set the oven to 200°C, 400°F, Gas Mark 6.
2. Poach the salmon in boiling, salted water and 1 tbsp of the lemon juice for 12 minutes. Remove with a spatula and cool.
3. Roll out the pastry and cut into 4 pieces, each slightly larger than a steak.
4. Place each steak on a pastry piece and smear with butter. Top with thin slices of cucumber and a pinch of dill weed (or fresh sprig if available). Season with salt and freshly ground black pepper. Dampen the edges of the remaining pastry pieces, place on top and pinch round the edges to seal.
5. Place on a greased baking tray, brush with milk and bake for 15-20 minutes until golden brown.
6. Meanwhile shred the remaining cucumber and stir in the sour cream, parsley, onion and remaining lemon juice. Heat gently, but do not boil. Season to taste and serve separately.

HOMARD HEBRIDEAN   *Serves 2*

This extravagant and tipsy treatment of lobster comes from the French chef of Cousteau's Restaurant, Hanover Street.

Metric		lb/oz	U.S.A.
	1 × 1-1½ kg (2-3 lb) Lobster, ready cooked		
50 g	*Butter*	2 oz	¼ cup
1	*Onion, chopped*	1	½ cup
125 g	*Mushrooms, sliced*	4 oz	1 cup
1	*Fresh mixed herbs, pinch of*	1	1
1	*Drambuie measure*	1	1
1	*Grated nutmeg, pinch of*	1	1
½ tsp	*English mustard*	½ tsp	½ tsp
150 ml	*Double cream*	¼ pt	½ cup
50 g	*Gruyère cheese, grated*	2 oz	½ cup
1 tbsp	*Whipped cream*	1 tbsp	1 tbsp
	Two truffles, tomato slices and chopped parsley to garnish		

1. Melt the butter in a large pan over a gentle heat. Add the onions and sauté until tender.
2. Remove the meat from the lobster shell. Chop the meat and add to the onion with the mushrooms and mixed herbs. Sauté for a few minutes.
3. Pour over the Drambuie and flambé.
4. Stir in the nutmeg and mustard, season to taste and pour in the double cream. Simmer until the sauce has thickened then check the seasoning.
5. Stir in the cheese and whipped cream.
6. Spoon the mixture into the lobster shells and glaze under the grill for a few minutes. Serve garnished with truffles, tomatoes and parsley.

OLD SMOKEY or 'Auld Reeky' are popular names for Edinburgh probably deriving not from the City's volcanic foundations, but from the bluey veil of smoke which hung over the Old Town in the days when people cooked on open fires.

ARTHUR'S SEAT, a well known high spot near to the summit of an extinct volcano probably derives its name not from the legendary king, but from its dominating position as an archer's seat. The road around it was built in the 19th century as part of a sort of early job creation scheme instituted by a radical politician of the time. The episode is referred to in the nursery rhyme:

'Round and round the Radical Rock
The Radical Rascal ran,
If you can tell me how many r's in that,
You'll be a clever man.'

BLUE STUART FILLET   *Serves 4*

Taking its name from its ingredients — blue cheese and Scottish beef — this rich combination comes from the King James Hotel.

Metric		lb/oz	U.S.A.
	4 × 200 g (7 oz) Fillet of prime Aberdeen Angus steak		
175 g	*Danish blue cheese, crumbled*	6 oz	1½ cups
50 g	*Butter*	2 oz	¼ cup
8	*Walnuts, shelled*	8	8
150 ml	*Madeira wine*	¼ pt	½ cup
150 ml	*Demi-glace sauce (see p.71)*	¼ pt	½ cup
	A small knob of butter for the sauce		

1. Make a slit in each fillet and stuff the meat with the cheese.
2. Melt the butter and cook the fillets to taste. Pour over the Madeira, then transfer the steaks to a warmed dish and top each one with a quartered walnut.
3. Reduce the Madeira to half, then add the demi-glace sauce.
4. Crush the remaining walnuts and add with a knob of butter. Simmer, stirring continuously, but do not boil.
5. When reduced and thickened, pour over the steaks and serve.

"After-dinner talk
Across the walnuts and the wine."   The Miller's Daughter
                    ALFRED, LORD TENNYSON, 1809-1892

THE CANONGATE 'S' MARKS

Set at intervals in the road, these marks indicate the boundary of sanctuary offered by Holyrood Abbey. Any debtor crossing the line was safe from his pursuers whilst within it. On Sundays he could

cross the line without fear of arrest. Thomson's Court, just beyond the line, was often used by the debtors, who at one time included De Quincey in their number.

CANONGATE TOLBOOTH

Built in the Franco-Scottish style in 1591, the projecting clock and stone dormers being Victorian additions, this striking building on the Royal Mile served as a council house, courtroom and jail of the Burgh of Canongate. It was also where dues or tolls were collected — hence the name. Today the Tolbooth is a museum and brass rubbing centre.

FILLET ELLERSLY   *Serves 2*

The chef of the Ellersly House Hotel has devised this simple but delicious way of making the most of steak.

Metric		*lb/oz*	*U.S.A.*
	2 × 225 g (8 oz) Fillet steaks		
50 g	Butter	2 oz	¼ cup
2	Slices of toast	2	2
125 g	Pâté	4 oz	½ cup
1	Onion, finely chopped	1	½ cup
1	Tomato, chopped	1	1
3	Mushrooms, sliced	3	3
10	Green peppercorns	10	10
2 tbsp	Red wine	2 tbsp	2 tbsp
150 ml	Double cream	¼ pt	½ cup

1. Melt half the butter in a pan and fry the steaks.
2. When cooked remove from the pan and place on the toast. Spread the pâté on top of the steaks. Keep warm.
3. Melt the remaining butter in the pan and add the onion, tomato, mushrooms and peppercorns. Sauté for half a minute then stir in the wine and cream.
4. Simmer until the liquid has thickened, but do not boil. Season to taste.
5. Put the steaks under a hot grill for a minute, transfer to warmed plates and coat with the sauce.

ENTRECOTE STEAK GLEN ISLA   *Serves 4*

An easy-to-follow recipe from Chef Sneden of the Rutland Hotel's Le Jardin Restaurant.

Metric		*lb/oz*	*U.S.A.*
	4 × 225 g (8 oz) Sirloin steaks		
4	Tomatoes	4	4
50 g	Butter	2 oz	¼ cup
175 g	Mushrooms, sliced	6 oz	2 cups
1 tsp	Rosemary	1 tsp	1 tsp
300 ml	Red wine	½ pt	1 cup

1. Season the steak on both sides with salt and pepper.
2. Skin the tomatoes by plunging into boiling water for a few moments — the skins will then come off easily. Quarter, de-seed and chop roughly to make a concasse.
3. Melt the butter in a pan and add the steak, mushrooms and rosemary. Cook for a few minutes on each side. Add the concasse and wine and cook until a thick sauce is produced.
4. Place the steak on a warm serving dish and pour a little of the sauce over. Serve any remaining sauce separately.

PORK SANDEMAN   *Serves 4*

A popular whisky-flamed dish from Nimmo's Restaurant.

Metric		lb/oz	U.S.A.
700 g	Pork fillet	1 ½ lb	1 ½ lb
2 tbsp	Flour	2 tbsp	2 tbsp
125 g	Clarified butter*	4 oz	½ cup
3 tbsp	Whisky	3 tbsp	¼ cup
600 ml	Double cream	1 pt	2 cups

1. Cut the pork into 12 escalopes and coat them in the flour. Fry gently in the butter in a large pan, turning once.
2. When cooked, pour over the whisky and flambé.
3. Add the cream and simmer until the liquid has reduced by half, but do not boil. Season, and serve at once.

To clarify butter, melt over a gentle heat. Remove and set aside until the milky solids settle. Skim the clarified butter from the top and transfer to a bowl. Cover and refrigerate until needed.

"Freedom and Whisky gang thegither!"
The Author's Earnest Cry and Prayer
ROBERT BURNS, 1759-1796

LAMB CUTLETS PERSILLE   *Serves 6*

Aileen Maguire of the Cringletie House Hotel finds this simple dish with its home-made sauce very popular.

Metric		lb/oz	U.S.A.
	12 Lamb cutlets		
300 ml	Home-made tomato sauce (see p.70)	½ pt	1 cup
225 g	Fresh breadcrumbs	8 oz	4 cups
1 tbsp	Parsley, freshly chopped	1 tbsp	1 tbsp
1	Garlic clove, crushed	1	1
1	Lemon, grated rind	1	1
1	Egg	1	1
4 tbsp	Milk	4 tbsp	⅓ cup
50 g	Flour	2 oz	½ cup

1. Set the oven to 180°C, 350°F, Gas Mark 4.
2. Make the tomato sauce and keep warm.
3. Mix the breadcrumbs, parsley, garlic and lemon rind. Season with salt and black pepper.
4. Beat the egg and milk together. Season the flour. Flour the cutlets and dip in egg mixture, then in breadcrumbs.
5. Cook under a hot grill on a greased baking tray until golden. Turn over and brown the other side.
6. Put in the oven until the cutlets are cooked through (about a further 10 minutes). Serve with the tomato sauce.

Kinloch Anderson

LORDE LVFE · GOD · ABOFE · AL · AND · YOVR · NYCHTBOVR · AS · YI · SELF ·

FOX

TIMBALE DE ROGNONS DIJONNAISE *Serves 4*

Even people who don't usually eat offal will rave over these rich and tasty vol-au-vents from Le Caveau.

Metric		lb/oz	U.S.A.
	4 Veal kidneys		
250 g	Puff pastry	8 oz	½ lb
1	Egg, beaten	1	1
1 tbsp	Oil	1 tbsp	1 tbsp
5	Onions, chopped	5	2½ cups
125 g	Mushrooms, sliced	4 oz	1 cup
2 tbsp	Brandy	2 tbsp	2 tbsp
150 ml	Red wine	¼ pt	½ cup
300 ml	Stock	½ pt	1 cup
2	Garlic cloves, crushed	2	2
1	Bouquet garni	1	1
30 g	Butter	1 oz	2 tbsp
30 g	Flour	1 oz	2 tbsp
2 tbsp	Dijon mustard	2 tbsp	2 tbsp

1. Set the oven to 210°C, 425°F, Gas Mark 7.
2. Roll out the pastry to 2 cm (¾") thick and cut out four vol-au-vent cases about 10 cm (4") diameter. With a smaller cutter cut an inner ring in the centre of each case, taking care to cut only half way through the pastry.
3. Place on a wetted baking tray and brush the tops with egg. Bake for about 10-15 minutes until golden brown, then remove lids and scoop out the soft insides.
4. Dice the kidneys removing the fat and cores.
5. Heat the oil in a pan and fry the kidneys on all sides turning them gently until browned all over. Add the onions and mushrooms and season. Strain off any fat. Pour the brandy over the kidneys and flambé.
6. Add the wine, stock, garlic and bouquet garni. Simmer for 20 minutes. Remove the kidneys and keep hot.
7. Bring the sauce to the boil and simmer until reduced by half. Thicken the sauce with a beurre manié (the flour worked into the butter) adding bit by bit.
9. Mix a little sauce with the mustard. Return to the sauce, stir well and then strain.
10. Stir in the kidneys and fill the vol-au-vents. Place the lids on top and heat through in a warm oven.

JOHN KNOX'S HOUSE

Dating back to 1490, this is one of the finest surviving medieval Edinburgh dwellings, and is now a museum containing John Knox memorabilia. He is said to have resided here between 1561 and 1572, and to have lectured passers-by from the steps on the virtues of religion. Threatened with demolition in the 18th century, the house was saved for posterity by an enraged public, and was bought by the Church of Scotland.

BIBLELAND takes its name from the inscription above the door. This one reads:
*'Behold how good a thing it is
  and how befitting well,
Together such as brethren are
  in unity to dwell,
'Tis an honour for men
  to cease from strife.'*

The tenement belonged to the Canongate Incorporation of Cordiners (shoemakers) — note the shoemakers' badge, a rounding knife, in the centre.

VEAU A LA LIMONE   *Serves 2*

We can guarantee that this delicious dish of veal from Denzler's which is served in a tangy wine sauce will be a soaraway success at dinner parties.

Metric		lb/oz	U.S.A.
	4 Thin veal slices		
50 g	Seasoned flour	2 oz	½ cup
	Oil for frying		
125 ml	White wine	4 fl. oz	½ cup
1	Lemon, juice of	1	1
25 g	Butter	1 oz	2 tbsp
	Lemon slices and parsley sprigs		

1. Flour the veal slices then fry in the oil for a minute on either side. Drain off the excess oil.
2. Pour the wine and lemon juice into the pan and add the butter.
3. Boil until the sauce thickens, turning the veal frequently.
4. Serve with lemon slices and parsley sprigs.

ROBERT LOUIS STEVENSON found inspiration for his novel about a spilt personality, 'Dr Jekyll and Mr Hyde', in the true story of a respectable Edinburgh councillor. Deacon Brodie's night-time activities were quite out of keeping with his day-time respectability. He burgled private houses and local buildings to supplement his gambling losses. But his double life was finally exposed and he was hanged on 1st October 1788 outside St Giles. His ghost is said to haunt the spot!

CHEESEY VEAL MADEIRA
Serves 4

The Parmesan coating gives a special flavour to this veal recipe from the Roxburghe Hotel, Charlotte Square.

Metric		lb/oz	U.S.A.
	4 × 175 g (6 oz) Veal escalopes		
2 tbsp	*Seasoned flour*	2 tbsp	2 tbsp
1	*Egg, beaten*	1	1
4 tbsp	*Parmesan cheese*	4 tbsp	⅓ cup
50 g	*Butter*	2 oz	¼ cup
4 tbsp	*Madeira*	4 tbsp	⅓ cup
175 g	*Mushrooms, sliced*	6 oz	2 cups
	Lemon slices and chopped parsley		

1. Coat the escalopes in flour. Brush with beaten egg, then coat with the Parmesan cheese.
2. Melt the butter in a large pan and sauté the veal for a few minutes on each side.
3. Pour the Madeira into the pan, add the mushrooms and finish cooking.
4. Transfer to a warm serving dish, pour over the sauce from the pan and garnish with the lemon slices and parsley.

THE MERCAT CROSS
Although always at the heart of Edinburgh, this ancient cross has changed its site over the years. In the 17th century it was at the commercial centre and was traditionally where transactions took place. It was at Mercat Cross that the death of James IV was announced, and also at its foot that Bonnie Prince Charlie proclaimed his exiled father King James III of England and VIII of Scotland.

CHICKEN SEVILLE   *Serves 2*

A fruity chicken treat from Denzler's.

Metric		lb/oz	U.S.A.
	2 × 225 g (8 oz) Chicken suprêmes		
60 g	*Gruyére cheese, chopped*	2 oz	½ cup
60 g	*Cooked ham, chopped*	2 oz	½ cup
2 tbsp	*Chopped parsley*	2 tbsp	2 tbsp
2 tbsp	*Seasoned flour*	2 tbsp	2 tbsp
1	*Egg, beaten*	1	1
60 g	*Fresh breadcrumbs*	2 oz	1 cup
	Oil for deep frying		
	For the sauce:		
1	*Orange, juice and grated rind, reserving 2 slices*	1	1
1	*Lemon, juice and grated rind, reserving 2 slices*	1	1
60 g	*Granulated sugar*	2 oz	¼ cup
60 g	*Brown sugar*	2 oz	½ cup
113 ml	*Bottled orange juice*	4 fl. oz	½ cup
2 tbsp	*Grand Marnier*	2 tbsp	2 tbsp
3	*Worcestershire sauce, dashes*	3	3
1 tbsp	*Cornflour*	1 tbsp	1 tbsp

1. Set the oven to 200°C, 400°F, Gas Mark 6.
2. Open out and flatten the suprêmes.
3. Mix the cheese, ham and parsley and divide the mixture between them. Fold in 'parcels', and coat in flour, egg and breadcrumbs.
4. Deep fry for a minute to seal, then bake for 10 minutes.
5. Boil 2 tsp of rind with the granulated sugar in 150 ml (¼ pt, ½ cup) water for 5 minutes.
6. In another pan, dissolve the brown sugar in the fruit juices. Add the liqueur, Worcester sauce and rind syrup.
7. Mix the cornflour with a little water and add to the sauce. Bring to the boil, stirring continuously, to thicken.
8. Transfer the chicken to a serving dish, pour over the sauce and garnish with the orange and lemon slices.

CHICKEN TROPICANA   *Serves 2*

Filipino Chef, Paul Subido, has created this succulent fruity treatment of chicken for Nimmo's Restaurant.

Metric		lb/oz	U.S.A.
	1 × 1 kg (2 lb) Chicken		
50 g	Clarified butter (see p.31)	2 oz	¼ cup
2	Garlic cloves, crushed	2	2
150 ml	Wine vinegar	¼ pt	½ cup
2	Bananas	2	2
125 g	Flaked almonds	4 oz	1 cup
1	Lemon	1	1
2	Melon slices	2	2

1. Split the bird down the breastbone opening each piece.
2. Melt the butter in a flat pan, allow to cool slightly, and use a little to brush the chicken. Grill until almost cooked.
3. Mix the garlic and vinegar and brush over the chicken. Finish cooking, then transfer to a platter and keep warm.
4. Cut the bananas in thick, slanting slices. Re-heat the butter and fry them briefly until brown. Place around the chicken.
5. Toss the almonds in the pan and add the juice of half the lemon. Heat through gently, and pour over the chicken.
6. Cut the remaining half of the lemon into wedges, place around the chicken with the melon slices and serve at once.

STOVED HOWTOWDIE   *Serves 4*

Which came first, the chicken or the egg? Don't worry — they're both in this traditional dish from the Ellersly House Hotel.

Metric		lb/oz	U.S.A.
	1 × 2 kg (4 lb) Chicken, cooked		
4	Large potatoes, sliced	4	4
2	Onions, halved and sliced	2	2
1 litre	Chicken stock	2 pt	4 cups
4	Eggs	4	4
3 tbsp	Parsley, chopped	3 tbsp	¼ cup

1. Set the oven to 150°C, 300°F, Gas Mark 2.
2. Cut the chicken into eight. Lay in a deep ovenproof dish.
3. Put the potatoes and onions on top, add the stock, season with salt and pepper and bake for about an hour until the potatoes are cooked.
4. Poach the eggs. Arrange on top of the chicken and potatoes, sprinkle with the parsley and serve at once.

LATIN MOTTO, HUNTLY HOUSE MUSEUM
Huntly House in Canongate is known as 'the speaking house' because of the 16th century Latin mottos along its front. This one translates 'Today for me, tomorrow for thee, why therefore carest thou?'.

WHITE HORSE CLOSE

This delightful little court owes its name to the 17th century inn and coaching stables. In its turn, the inn is rumoured to have been named after Mary Queen of Scots' much adored white palfrey. It was also a favourite haunt of Bonnie Prince Charlie's Jacobite officers. In days gone by, travellers could catch the London stagecoach here.

CHICKEN CRAIGELLACHLE   *Serves 4*

Prime Scottish ingredients — redcurrants, honey and whisky — feature in this recipe from Chef Mackay of the Post House.

Metric		*lb/oz*	*U.S.A.*
	4 × 175 g (6 oz) Chicken suprêmes		
3 tbsp	*Flour*	3 tbsp	¼ cup
125 g	*Butter*	4 oz	½ cup
2	*Onions, chopped*	2	1 cup
4 tbsp	*Whisky*	4 tbsp	⅓ cup
125 g	*Clear honey*	4 oz	⅓ cup
300 ml	*Double cream*	½ pt	1 cup
125 g	*Redcurrants*	4 oz	½ cup

1. Coat the chicken in the flour seasoned with salt and pepper.
2. Melt the butter in a pan and gently cook the chicken but do not allow to brown.
3. Add the onion and cook gently for a few minutes.
4. Pour over the whisky and flambé.
5. Stir in the honey and cream then simmer for 5-8 minutes.
6. Add the redcurrants just before serving to heat through.
7. Transfer the chicken to a warm serving dish and coat with the redcurrant sauce.

"Curses are like chickens; they come home to roost."
14th century proverb

HAUNCH OF VENISON
BONNIE PRINCE CHARLIE   *Serves 2*

Metric		*lb/oz*	*U.S.A.*
	2 × 175 g (6 oz) Venison steaks		
2 tbsp	*Flour*	2 tbsp	2 tbsp
50 g	*Butter*	2 oz	¼ cup
2	*Onions, finely chopped*	2	1 cup
4	*Mushrooms, sliced*	4	½ cup
4 tbsp	*Drambuie*	4 tbsp	⅓ cup
200 ml	*Single cream*	⅓ pt	¾ cup
2 tbsp	*Parsley, chopped*	2 tbsp	2 tbsp

No Edinburgh cookbook would be complete without a venison recipe — this one also makes use of the Scottish liqueur, Drambuie, and is served in Le Jardin Restaurant.

1. Cut the venison into slices about 2 cm (¾") thick. Season with salt and pepper and dust on both sides with flour.
2. Melt the butter in a pan and shallow fry the fillets with the onions and mushrooms. (The venison should not be overcooked.)
3. Pour over the Drambuie and flambé.
4. Add the cream and cook over a gentle heat until the cream is reduced and a delicious creamy sauce is produced.
5. Place on a warm serving dish and garnish with parsley.

"Charlie is my darling, my darling, my darling,
Charlie is my darling, the young Chevalier."

Charlie is my Darling
LADY NAIRNE, 1766-1845

THE HIGH KIRK OF ST GILES

St Giles' Kirk is often mistakenly described as a cathedral. In 1633, Charles I's efforts to make it one led to a furious row, culminating in the notorious occasion when one Jenny Geddes hurled her stool at the Dean's head!

St Giles is 206 feet long and 129 feet wide, and sports an ornate crown added when the Pope declared it a collegiate church in 1467. During the 17th and 18th centuries, it suffered the indignity of being split into four, daily services were suspended, and the building was used for secular purposes — there was even a police station in the nave!

It reverted to one church in 1884, and is today
recognised as the most important ecclesiastical
building in Edinburgh. Visitors and worshippers
alike can enjoy its Gothic splendour, and reflect
upon its history as a place of worship and a
monument to political and religious activities.

Scholarly Foundations

*"For there was never yet philosopher
That could endure the toothache patiently."*

Much Ado About Nothing
WILLIAM SHAKESPEARE, 1564-1616

John Knox, 1505-1572

Renowned not least for his out-spokeness against the monarchy, this statue of the great preacher now stands inside St Giles Kirk. He dedicated his life to establishing the Protestant faith in Scotland improving educational systems in both schools and universities, and aiding the poor. He is thought to have been born in 1505, and died in 1572.

Knox was at the height of his powers and influence when the Catholic Mary Queen of Scots arrived from France to claim the Scottish throne. Understandably, there was a violent clash of personalities and of interests between the two!

David Hume, 1711-1776

This outstanding philosopher was notorious among Edinburgh's ardent Protestant townspeople for his philosophical atheism. Indeed, he was denied a professorship at the university because of it. The story is told that Hume once fell into a shallow bog and was told by the woman passer-by from whom he asked assistance to first denounce his atheism. Apparently he stoutly refused to do this. Unfortunately the story does not relate how he finally got out of the bog!

Adam Smith, 1723-1790

This famous political economist and author of "The Wealth Of Nations", lived in Canongate and is buried in Canongate Kirk. He was the first to 'coin' the phrase 'a nation of shopkeepers' as a description of the British!

Edinburgh University

Along with its royal and religious associations Edinburgh has long had a first class reputation as a centre of learning.
James VI established the university in 1583 under Royal

DANIEL STEWART'S AND MELVILLE COLLEGE

Motorists travelling along the Queensferry Road should look out for this impressive building with lawns stretching down to the road. The original design was for a new Houses of Parliament in Westminster. Sadly for the architect, the design came second in the competition, but it must have been some consolation when he was asked to scale down the design to build this school. Its oriental-looking domes have, somewhat unkindly, earned it the nickname amongst schoolboys of 'the Taj Mahal'!

Charter making Edinburgh's the sixth oldest university in Great Britain. 1983 marked its 400th anniversary. Among students who later became famous are Sir Arthur Conan Doyle, Charles Darwin and Robert Louis Stevenson.

Despite its revered traditions and high academic standards, the history of the university is dotted with curios! For example, the discipline underwhich the students lived was rigorous and unyielding — they were forbidden to attend public executions in the Grassmarket since such occasions, accompanied as they were by street sellers and strolling players, were considered far too light-hearted for studious young men. They were not even allowed to attend funerals!

THE HEART OF MIDLOTHIAN

Set in the cobbles outside St Giles, this marks the site of the Old Tolbooth doorway. Many men later to die for their faith were imprisoned here. From this heart Sir Walter Scott took the title of his famous novel immortalising the storming of the Old Tolbooth prison in 1736.

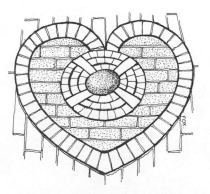

LAPIN ROTI AU MIEL *Serves 2-3*

An unusual rabbit dish from Chef Martelat of l'Auberge Restaurant Français.

Metric		lb/oz	U.S.A.
1 kg	Fresh rabbit, skinned with neck, back and hind legs in one piece	2½ lb	2½ lb
2 tbsp	Olive oil	2 tbsp	2 tbsp
1	Onion, very small cubes	1	½ cup
2	Carrots, very small cubes	2	1 cup
1 tsp	Fresh rosemary, chopped (or ½ tsp dried)	1 tsp	1 tsp
4 tbsp	Clear honey	4 tbsp	⅓ cup
150 ml	Veal or chicken stock	¼ pt	½ cup

1. Set the oven to 200°C, 400°F, Gas Mark 6.
2. Place the rabbit in a roasting tin and brush lightly with the oil. Season with salt, pepper and rosemary. Add 150 ml (¾ pt, ½ cup) of water and the mire poix (the onion and carrot cubes). Roast for about an hour, turning every ten minutes.
3. Ten minutes before the end of the cooking time, spread the rabbit with honey on all sides. Replace in the oven to finish cooking, then remove the rabbit from the tin. Joint the rabbit and keep warm.
4. Place the roasting tin on a high heat and reduce the cooking liquid to a syrup. Add the stock and a little water and season to taste. Stir in up to 1 tbsp of honey and cook until you have a smooth, shiny sauce.
5. Coat the rabbit joints in the sauce and serve with rice.

CREPES SURPRISES

*Serves 4 as a main course
or 8 as a starter*

This flexible dish from Le Caveau is suitable as a starter or main course. As a starter it will serve up to eight (according to appetites!), while served with salad as a main course it makes a nice lunch for four.

Metric		lb/oz	U.S.A.
	For the pancakes:		
125 g	Flour	4 oz	1 cup
3	Eggs, beaten	3	3
300 ml	Hot milk	½ pt	1 cup
2 tbsp	Oil for the batter	2 tbsp	2 tbsp
	Oil for frying		
	For the duxelles:		
15 g	Butter	½ oz	1 tbsp
250 g	Mushrooms, chopped	8 oz	2 cups
1	Onion, finely chopped	1	½ cup
2	Shallots, finely chopped	2	2
2 tbsp	Parsley, finely chopped	2 tbsp	2 tbsp
1	Nutmeg, pinch of	1	1
	For the sauce:		
25 g	Butter	¾ oz	1 tbsp
25 g	Flour	¾ oz	1 tbsp
300 ml	Milk	½ pt	1 cup
150 ml	Cream	¼ pt	½ cup
	For the topping:		
3 tbsp	Red Cheddar, grated	3 tbsp	¼ cup

1. Sift the flour into a bowl and stir in the beaten eggs. Season then pour on the hot milk and oil.
2. Beat the batter thoroughly, then refrigerate for 1-2 hours.
3. Heat the oil in a frying pan and make 8-10 thin pancakes placing inside a folded tea towel until needed.
4. For the duxelles, melt the butter in a pan and fry the mushrooms, onion, shallots and parsley until all the liquid has evaporated and the mixture is cooked. Season well and add the nutmeg.
5. To make the sauce, stir the butter and flour together in a pan over a low heat. Slowly stir in the milk and cream, beating well all the time until the mixture thickens, and season to taste. Remove from the heat.
6. Fill and roll each pancake neatly and place in a warmed ovenproof dish.
7. Cover the pancakes with the sauce, sprinkle the cheese on top and grill until golden brown and bubbling.

"No eggs! No eggs!! Thousand thunders, man, what do you mean by no eggs?" Saint Joan
GEORGE BERNARD SHAW, 1856-1950

LADY STAIR'S HOUSE

Hidden around a corner in the Landmarket (lawnmarket) area of the Royal Mile is this intriguing building which was constructed in 1662. It owes its name to the Countess of Stair, a dazzling beauty and leader of high fashion who took over the premises in the 18th century. It is now open as a museum and holds a fascinating collection of memorabilia from the three greats of Scottish literature — Robert Burns, Sir Walter Scott and Robert Louis Stevenson.

VIRGINIA CHICKEN AND APPLE SALAD   *Serves 6*

Crunchy and colourful ingredients in a creamy sauce turn everyday chicken into something special in this recipe from Hilda Nimmo of Nimmo's Restaurant.

Metric		lb/oz	U.S.A.
	1 × 1½ kg (3 lb) Chicken, cooked		
1	Lettuce	1	1
1	Chicory head	1	1
4 tbsp	Mayonnaise	4 tbsp	⅓ cup
150 ml	Double cream	¼ pt	½ cup
5 tbsp	Lemon juice	5 tbsp	5 tbsp
500 g	Red apples	1 lb	1 lb
1	Celery head, thinly sliced	1	1
12	Stuffed olives, thinly sliced	12	12
90 g	Flaked almonds	3 oz	1 cup

1. Remove the bones from the chicken and dice the meat into small pieces.
2. Wash the lettuce and chicory and arrange the lettuce on a large flat serving dish.
3. Blend the mayonnaise with the cream and 3 tbsp lemon juice. Season to taste.
4. Reserving one apple for decoration, quarter and core the remainder and toss in lemon juice.
5. Toss the chicken, apples, celery, olives and almonds in the mayonnaise until well coated and spoon into the centre of the lettuce.
6. Core the remaining apple and slice into rings, dipping them in the remaining lemon juice to prevent discoloration.
7. Tuck chicory leaves in the centre of each apple ring and use as a garnish.

"The sweetest hours that e'er I spend,
Are spent among the lasses O!"

Green grow the Rashes
ROBERT BURNS, 1759-1796

"Edina! Scotia's darling seat"   ROBERT BURNS, 1759-1796
On Edinburgh

"This profusion of eccentricities, this dream of masonry and living rock, not a drop scene in a theatre, but a city in the world of everyday reality."
ROBERT LOUIS STEVENSON, 1850-1894
On Edinburgh

THE CITY VIEWED FROM CALTON HILL

In itself a curious place, offering a hotch-potch of isolated monuments, memorials and buildings — most of them classical in style and even copied from Greek originals — Calton Hill provides the visitor with sweeping views of the City. It is an excellent spot from which to contemplate Edinburgh's growth, composition and architectural styles from different periods of history.

The Dugald Stewart monument seen here on the right is in the style of a small circular temple, and is dedicated to a former Professor of Moral Philosophy at Edinburgh University.

"Mine own romantic town"
SIR WALTER SCOTT, 1771-1832
On Edinburgh

CITY ARTS SALADS

Serves 4

The City Arts Centre Café specialises in salads — these three
are very popular. The first two go well with baked potatoes,
while the Special makes an excellent accompaniment to pork.

Green bean and mushroom salad

*"An attachment à la Plato for a bashful young potato, or a
not-too-French French bean."*   Patience, I
SIR W.S. GILBERT, 1836-1911

Metric		lb/oz	U.S.A.
250 g	French beans, fresh or frozen	8 oz	2 cups
250 g	Mushrooms, thinly sliced	8 oz	2 cups
3 tbsp	Mayonnaise	3 tbsp	¼ cup
½ tbsp	Horseradish sauce	½ tbsp	½ tbsp
	Black pepper, freshly ground		
½ tsp	Paprika	½ tsp	½ tsp

1. Cook the beans in salted, boiling water until just tender.
   Strain and leave to cool.
2. Wash and drain the mushrooms and mix with the beans.
3. Add the mayonnaise, horseradish and pepper and stir well.
4. Sprinkle with a little paprika before serving.

Crunchy cream cheese salad

Metric		lb/oz	U.S.A.
300 g	Natural yoghurt	10 oz	1¼ cups
300 g	Cream cheese	10 oz	1¼ cups
50 g	Cheese, grated	2 oz	½ cup
200 g	Sweetcorn, can of	7 oz	7 oz
6	Celery sticks, chopped	6	1½ cups
50 g	Walnuts, chopped	2 oz	½ cup
1 tbsp	Mango chutney (optional)	1 tbsp	1 tbsp
1	Lettuce	1	1
1 tbsp	Parsley, chopped	1 tbsp	1 tbsp

1. Gradually stir the yoghurt into the cream cheese.
2. Stir in the cheese, drained sweetcorn, celery and walnuts.
   If desired, add the chutney at this stage.
3. Serve on lettuce, sprinkled with parsley.

City Arts Special

Metric		lb/oz	U.S.A.
250 g	Kidney beans	8 oz	2 cups
2	Red peppers	2	2
3	Green dessert apples	3	3

2 tbsp	Fresh parsley, chopped	2 tbsp	2 tbsp
	For the dressing:		
3 tbsp	Oil (olive if you feel extravagant!)	3 tbsp	¼ cup
1 tbsp	Wine vinegar	1 tbsp	1 tbsp
1 tbsp	Tomato purée	1 tbsp	1 tbsp
¼ tsp	Garlic powder	¼ tsp	¼ tsp

1. Soak the kidney beans overnight in at least 600 ml (1 pt, 2½ cups) water.
2. Next day, drain and rinse the beans. Put into a large pan and cover with boiling water. Bring up to the boil then boil gently for at least one hour until tender. Strain, rinse and leave to cool.
3. Mix the dressing ingredients well and pour over the beans.
4. De-seed the peppers and cut into long thin strips. Core and slice the apples. Stir the peppers and apples into the beans and sprinkle with parsley.

NIMMO'S PICKLED CUCUMBER

Metric		lb/oz	U.S.A.
1	Cucumber	1	1
150 ml	White vinegar	¼ pt	½ cup
125 g	Caster sugar	4 oz	½ cup
5	Peppercorns	5	5
1	Onion, thinly sliced	1	1 cup

1. Slice the cucumber thinly and place in a shallow dish.
2. Mix the vinegar, sugar, peppercorns and onion together with 150 ml (¼ pt, ½ cup) of water.
3. Pour over the cucumber and refrigerate overnight. Serve chilled.

GYPSY POTATOES   Serves 6

A tasty vegetable contribution from the Cringletie House Hotel.

Metric		lb/oz	U.S.A.
1 kg	Potatoes	2 lb	2 lb
400 g	Tomatoes, can of	14 oz	14 oz
50 g	Butter or margarine	2 oz	¼ cup
125 g	Cheddar cheese, grated	4 oz	1 cup

1. Set the oven to 180°C, 350°F, Gas Mark 4.
2. Peel and slice the potatoes thinly into cold water.
3. Mash the tomatoes with the juice.
4. Butter an ovenproof dish. Layer the potatoes, tomatoes, grated cheese and salt and pepper, finishing with a layer of cheese, then dot with the remaining butter.
5. Cover and bake for one hour or until cooked, removing the cover for the last 10 minutes to brown the top slightly.

PEACH HIGHLAND CREAM   *Serves 4*

This Caledonian Hotel dessert has a strong Scottish flavour!

Metric		lb/oz	U.S.A.
4	Peaches	4	4
5 tbsp	Whisky	5 tbsp	7 tbsp
125 g	Sugar	4 oz	½ cup
4	Raspberry sorbet, scoops	4	4
2	Egg yolks	2	2
60 g	Choux pastry (See p.70)	2 oz	2 oz
1	Dessert apple	1	1
2 tbsp	Lemon juice	2 tbsp	2 tbsp
150 ml	Double cream	¼ pt	½ cup

1. Peel the peaches* and place them in a pan with 1 tbsp of the whisky, half the sugar and 300 ml (½ pt, 1 cup) water.
2. Bring to the boil then reduce the heat and simmer gently to poach the peaches until they are tender.
3. Drain and cool the peaches, then halve and stone them.
4. Fill with sorbet and place the halves together again. Transfer each peach to the bottom of a tall glass.
5. Put the egg yolks and remaining sugar and whisky in a bain marie (or a basin over a pan of hot water). Beat well until the mixture doubles in volume and you can see whisk marks in the sauce. Divide between the glasses.
6. Make 'S' swans' necks from choux pastry (these can be made in advance and kept in the freezer until required).
7. Slice the apple into segments and core. Dip in lemon juice to prevent discoloration. These slices become the swans' tails. Arrange the swans' necks and tails on the glasses.
8. Whip the cream and spoon into the centre of the glasses.

* If the skins are difficult to remove, plunge in boiling water for a few moments — Editor.

RASPBERRY SORBET   *Serves 4*

If you have time to make your own raspberry sorbet for the dessert opposite, here's a good recipe. Frozen raspberries may be used.

Metric		lb/oz	U.S.A.
500 g	*Raspberries*	1 lb	1 lb
50 g	*Sugar*	2 oz	¼ cup
1	*Lemon, juice of*	1	1
½ tsp	*Vanilla essence*	½ tsp	½ tsp
2	*Egg whites*	2	2

1. Turn the refrigerator thermostat to its coldest setting.
2. Place the raspberries in a liquidizer or blender and blend until you have a purée. Do this in two stages if necessary.
3. Pour the purée into a measuring jug and top up with a little water until you have 600 ml (1 pt, 2½ cups) of liquid.
4. Pour into a large mixing bowl and stir in the sugar. Add the lemon juice and vanilla essence and beat well.
5. Whisk the egg whites until stiff, then fold them into the raspberry mixture until it is smooth.
6. Pour the mixture into a freezer tray and place in the freezer.
7. After about 30 minutes, when the mixture has started to set around the edges, remove from the freezer and place in the mixing bowl. Beat until smooth then return to the freezer tray and freeze for a further 3 hours.
8. Use a spoon dipped in hot water to spoon out the mixture.

EDINBURGH FOG   *Serves 8*

This aptly named creamy dessert is simple to make and delicious. The recipe comes from the Rutland Hotel's Le Jardin Restaurant.

Metric		lb/oz	U.S.A.
900 ml	*Double cream*	1½ pt	3 cups
	Caster sugar		
	Vanilla essence		
250 g	*Ratafia biscuits or praline, crushed*	8 oz	2 cups
50 g	*Blanched, split almonds*	2 oz	½ cup

1. Beat the cream until fairly stiff adding a little sugar and vanilla to taste.*
2. Stir in the ratafias or praline and pile into individual glass dishes.
3. Toast the almonds under the grill until lightly brown and sprinkle on top.

* Some Scots add a little whisky at this stage — Editor.

54

These two recipes come from Denzler's in Queen Street — the first one doesn't contain cheese, it comes from the Gruyère region.

BANANES A LA GRUYERE   Serves 2

Metric		lb/oz	U.S.A.
	2 Bananas		
1 tbsp	Granulated sugar	1 tbsp	1 tbsp
4	Macaroons	4	4
2 tbsp	Maraschino	2 tbsp	2 tbsp
2 tbsp	Apricot jam	2 tbsp	2 tbsp
1 tbsp	Kirsch	1 tbsp	1 tbsp
125 ml	Double cream, whipped	4 fl. oz	½ cup
25 g	Grated chocolate	1 oz	1 square

1. Place 4 tbsp water in a small pan with the sugar and heat until the sugar has dissolved to make a syrup.
2. Soak the macaroons in the Maraschino and 2 tbsp syrup.
3. Mix the jam, Kirsch and remaining stock syrup.
4. Slice the bananas and mix into the jam mixture.
5. Place a macaroon in each dessert glass, divide the banana mixture equally and top with macaroons.
6. Pipe the cream on top and sprinkle with chocolate.

SABAYON GLACEE AU VIN BLANC   Serves 8

Metric		lb/oz	U.S.A.
150 ml	White wine	¼ pt	½ cup
175 g	Caster sugar	6 oz	¾ cup
6	Egg yolks	6	6
2	Gelatine leaves*	2	2
600 ml	Double cream	1 pt	2½ cups

1. Put the wine and sugar in a saucepan and bring slowly to the boil stirring all the time. Remove from the heat.
2. Whip the egg yolks until thick and then beat into the boiled wine, continuing to beat until the mixture is cold and stiff.
3. Dissolve the gelatine in a little warm water, then stir in.
4. Whip the cream stiffly and fold half into the mixture.
5. Divide between the dishes and refrigerate. Pipe with cream before serving.

* or 1 packet — Editor.

THE YOUNG QUEEN OF SCOTS is popularly supposed to have bathed in white wine! Queen Mary's Bath House is a small building just off the Abbey Strand at the bottom of the Royal Mile!

BUTTERSCOTCH VELVET
Serves 6

Scottish butterscotch candy is world famous, so this Cringletie House dessert will no doubt be very popular too.

Metric		lb/oz	U.S.A.
50 g	*Butter*	2 oz	¼ cup
50 g	*Brown sugar*	2 oz	¼ cup
1 tbsp	*Golden syrup*	1 tbsp	1 tbsp
2 tbsp	*Cornflour*	2 tbsp	2 tbsp
500 ml	*Milk*	1 pt	2½ cups

1. Melt the butter, sugar and syrup in a large pan and bring to the boil. Remove from the heat.
2. Mix the cornflour with a little of the milk. Bring the rest of the milk to the boil in a separate pan.
3. Pour the hot milk over the syrup mixture and bring back to the boil. Add the cornflour and continue stirring. When thick and creamy set aside to cool, covering to prevent a skin forming. Pour into a dish and cover again.
4. This can be served cold, decorated with whipped cream but is also delicious served warm with pouring cream.

BANANES AU RHUM ET CAFÉ
Serves 4

This luscious concoction from Cousteau's Restaurant is fit for the angels, but could the fact that it calls for 'cat's tongue' biscuits have anything to do with our footnote?

Metric		lb/oz	U.S.A.
8	*Bananas*	8	8
600 ml	*Strong coffee*	1 pt	2 cups
225 g	*Sugar*	8 oz	1 cup
50 ml	*Dark rum*	3 tbsp	¼ cup
300 ml	*Double cream*	½ pt	1 cup
4	*Langues du chat (sponge fingers)*	4	4

1. Place the coffee and sugar in a heavy pan and bring to the boil. Stir continuously until the mixture is reduced to a third. Set aside to cool.
2. Slice the bananas and divide between four glasses.
3. Stir the rum into the coffee, pour over the bananas and place in the refrigerator to chill for one hour.
4. Whip the double cream until thick then decorate the top of the coffee and bananas.
5. Decorate with the sponge finger biscuits and serve at once.

BUBBLE, BUBBLE, TOIL AND TROUBLE! It didn't always pay to create new recipes — at Witches' Corner on Castle Esplanade a little iron well marks the spot where, between 1479 and 1722, over 300 women were burnt at the stake for supposed witchcraft.

Science & the Arts

Science and technology have long benefitted from the efforts and abilities of Edinburgh men, among them:

Alexander Graham Bell, 1847-1922
The pioneer of the telephone was born at 16 South Charlotte Street, went to the old Royal High School and then attended Edinburgh University.

Lord Lister, 1827-1918
We have Joseph Lister to thank for antiseptic. He pioneered the use of carbolic acid to prevent wounds going septic, and his efforts earned him the first medical peerage.

Sir James Young Simpson, 1811-1870
Simpson was the first man to investigate the use of chloroform in surgery. History has it that he first tried it out on his own dinner guests. No doubt they ended up under the table!

John Logie Baird, 1883-1948
The inventor of the television did his early experimental work in a tenement in Edinburgh.

Charles Darwin, 1809-1882
Famous for 'The Origin Of Species', Darwin studied at the university, though not as an undergraduate.

CHARLOTTE SQUARE

In 1791 Robert Adam was commissioned by the authorities to design Charlotte Square. With the famous north side, shown here, he gave Edinburgh what has proved to be one of the finest and most well known street fronts in Europe. Behind the spectacular facade, designed to resemble a great palace, are eleven houses. Although many are now offices, the overall illusion is largely perpetuated.

Named after George III's wife, Queen Charlotte, this famous Square has had some equally renowned residents. Among them have been Joseph Lister, the antiseptics pioneer at number 9; William Fettes, founder of Edinburgh's famous school at number 13; and Earl Haig, the First World War General at number 24. Alexander Graham Bell, the inventor of the telephone, was born in South Charlotte Street, at number 16.

58

The Arts have also had their share of Edinburgh Greats. Here are just a few.

James Boswell, 1740-1795

A local man, his fame rests almost entirely on his biography of Dr. Johnson. It is said that he used to follow the great man around to the extent of making himself quite a nuisance. Still, it must be said that Dr. Johnson's fame was certainly enhanced by Boswell's book about him!

Robert Burns, 1759-1796

Notorious for his romantic dalliances and remembered for his lyrical love poetry, Scots celebrate his birthday each year on Burns' Night. Burns' Supper is an occasion of feasting and merry-making, and one can imagine that Burns himself would have heartily approved!

'Robbie Burns' is Scotland's most loved poet. He came from a modest country family in Ayrshire, but emerged from his rural backwater to become the darling of Edinburgh society.

In literary terms his poetry was innovative and daring. Not for Burns the classical codes of theme and style. Instead he embraced all sorts of flesh and blood subjects (particularly wine, women and song!) and wrote about them in his local dialect. Far from repulsing sophisticated tastes, Burns' frankness delighted the fashionable circles.

Robert Louis Stevenson, 1850-1894

17 Heriot Row was the home of one of Edinburgh's most popular novelists during his childhood and student days.

Robert Louis Stevenson was a sickly child and confined to his bed where his vivid creative imagination kept him amused. Despite his delicate health and middle class upbringing, he grew up to be a rebellious young man, seeking the company of more colourful, if less respectable characters in the seedier parts of Edinburgh!

No doubt this experience fed the imagination which brought us such chilling characters as Long John Silver in Treasure Island.

> *"There is no duty we so much underrate as the duty of being happy."*

Daniel Defoe, 1661-1731

Publicly Defoe was a novelist and journalist. Although English, he edited a newspaper called 'The Edinburgh Courant'. He

wrote of Edinburgh, in his notes on travelling in Britain, about the risk 'if you walk the streets, of having chamber-pots of ordure thrown upon your head'!
Privately, Defoe worked as a government spy, investigating the local feeling towards the Act of Union between Scotland and England in 1707.

Oliver Goldsmith, 1728-1774
The 18th century novelist was a medical student at Edinburgh University. However, he is not noted for any outstanding contributions to medical science — he is said to have been more interested in ladies than studies!

Sir Henry Raeburn, 1756-1823
Sir Walter Scott was just one of Raeburn's famous sitters. A member of Edinburgh's élite social circles, he recorded many famous faces of his day. A list of his portrait subjects is rather like a 'Who's Who' of Georgian Edinburgh.

Sir Walter Scott, 1771-1832
Sir Walter Scott was largely responsible for the 19th century Romantic fascination with all things Scottish.
He was a respected lawyer but his lasting reputation as an internationally recognized author came with his prolific production of romantic novels: The Heart of Midlothian, Rob Roy, Redgauntlet to name just three.
Contemporary history provided him with all the ingredients for gripping adventure stories: war, rebellion, martyrdom and tragic love. Although he turned to English history for Ivanhoe, his passion was always for the tales of his native Scotland.

Arthur Conan Doyle, 1859-1930
Although Sherlock Holmes is commonly associated with Baker Street in London, his creator Sir Arthur Doyle was born and educated in Edinburgh, studying at the university.

Kenneth Grahame, 1859-1932
The author of 'Wind in the Willows', popular with children and adults alike, was born at 32 Castle Street. Surely Badger must have been based on some dour old Scotsman he had known in his youth!

Muriel Spark, born 1918
Edinburgh does not only boast literary figures from the past: Muriel Spark was educated here at the 'James Gillespie's High School For Girls', which she immortalised in her popular novel 'The Prime of Miss Jean Brodie'.

Mary Stewart, born 1916
Best known for her Arthurian trilogy 'The Crystal Cave', 'The Hollow Hills', and 'The Last Enchantment', the novelist Mary Stewart has lived in Edinburgh for many years.

THE ROYAL SCOTS GREY'S MEMORIAL AND THE OLD TOWN

Who can walk along Princes Street without being struck by this outstanding monument to the men of the regiment, now known as the Royal Scots Dragoon Guards, who died in the Boer War and two World Wars?

This view from Princes Street Gardens shows the spikey skyline of the Old Town with its rooftops, turrets and spires. The twin towers in the centre belong to Playfair's Free Church Assembly Hall built in 1861. To its right is the massive spire of Gillespie Graham's Tolbooth Church, built in 1844. Its spire is 73 metres high, the tallest in Edinburgh. It was also unusual in that its Sunday afternoon services used to be held entirely in Gaelic! They are now held in Greyfriars.

At the far right can be seen the turrets of Ramsay House, built in 1740 by the poet Allan Ramsay. The curious octagonal shape of the building led local wits to liken it to a 'goose-pie'. It is reported that Mr Ramsay was not amused, but nonetheless it is often now referred to as Goosepie House.

ORANGE CHEESECAKE

Serves 4-6

Even dieters might allow themselves a sliver of this light, cottage cheese based delight from Cringletie House Hotel.

Metric		lb/oz	U.S.A.
1 pkt	Gelatine	1 pkt	1 pkt
150 ml	Concentrated orange juice	¼ pt	½ cup
1	Egg, separated	1	1
50 g	Caster sugar	2 oz	¼ cup
375 g	Cottage cheese, sieved	12 oz	1½ cups
1	Orange, grated rind and segments	1	1
150 ml	Double cream	¼ pt	½ cup
125 g	Biscuit crumbs	4 oz	1 cup

1. Soak the gelatine in the juice for ten minutes. Heat gently, stirring continuously until dissolved. Cool a little.
2. Beat the egg yolk and half of the sugar together over a pan of hot water. When the mixture begins to thicken, stir in the gelatine mixture and a pinch of salt. Set aside to cool.
3. Blend the cottage cheese and orange rind into the gelatine mixture. Then whip the cream and fold this in.
4. Beat the egg white until stiff, add the remaining sugar and re-whip until shiny.
5. Fold the egg white gently and quickly into the gelatine mixture then turn into a wetted 18-20 cm (7"-8") loose-bottomed tin. When set, transfer to a plate, decorating the side with crumbs and top with orange segments.

BORDER TART   *Serves 8*

This traditional Scottish dish is served at teatime, coffee time
or to round off a meal. The recipe comes from Mrs. Betty
Boyd, an excellent Scottish cook who has run her own
teashop as well as feeding a sweet-toothed family.

Metric		lb/oz	U.S.A.
	For the pastry:		
175 g	*Plain flour*	6 oz	1½ cups
80 g	*Margarine or cooking fat*	3 oz	⅓ cup
	For the filling:		
40 g	*Margarine*	1½ oz	3 tbsp
80 g	*Sugar*	3 oz	⅓ cup
1	*Egg*	1	1
125 g	*Dried fruit, or a mixture of raisins, nuts and cherries*	4 oz	⅔ cup
	Almond essence to taste		
	For the topping:		
125 g	*Icing sugar, sifted*	4 oz	1 cup
1 tbsp	*Mixed nuts, chopped*	1 tbsp	1 tbsp

1. Set the oven to 180°C, 350°F, Gas Mark 4.
2. To make the pastry, sift the flour into a bowl and rub in the
   fat until the mixture resembles fine breadcrumbs. Add
   enough water to make a firm dough.
3. Roll out the pastry on a floured board and line a greased
   18 cm (7") flan tin. Refrigerate.
4. To make the filling, cream together the margarine and
   sugar until the mixture is light and fluffy.
5. Add the egg and beat well. Stir in the fruit and essence.
6. Pour the mixture into the pastry case and bake for 30
   minutes. When set, remove from the oven and allow to
   cool in the tin.
7. Mix the icing sugar with a few drops of cold water and beat
   well until the mixture is firm and smooth.
8. Remove the tart from the tin and spread the icing on top.
9. Scatter the nuts on top and leave to set before cutting.

"Promises and pie-crust are made to be broken."
Polite Conversation
JONATHAN SWIFT, 1667-1745

MANDARIN CREAM PIE   *Serves 6*

Metric		lb/oz	U.S.A.
	1 × 25 cm (10") Pastry case		
300 ml	*Custard*	½ pt	1 cup
200 g	*Mandarins, can of*	7 oz	7 oz
150 ml	*Double cream*	¼ pt	½ cup
50 g	*Plain chocolate, grated*	2 oz	2 squares

This 'instant' dessert from the City Arts Centre can also be made in a meringue shell or ready-made flan case for speed.

1. Make up the custard by following the instructions on the packet. When it thickens, set aside to cool.
2. When the custard is cool but has not set, stir in the drained mandarins.
3. Pour the mixture into the flan case and leave to set.
4. Whip the cream and spread over the top of the flan. Then sprinkle with the chocolate. Chill.

TARTE TATIN   *Serves 4-6*

There are strong historical connections between France and Scotland. Perhaps that's why this is a popular choice at Le Caveau.

Metric		lb/oz	U.S.A.
	For the shortcrust pastry:		
250 g	*Flour, sifted*	8 oz	2 cups
125 g	*Butter*	4 oz	½ cup
	For the filling:		
175 g	*Caster sugar*	6 oz	¾ cup
750 g	*Cooking apples, peeled and thinly sliced*	1½ lb	4 cups
50 g	*Butter*	2 oz	¼ cup

1. Set the oven to 180°C, 350°F, Gas Mark 4. Place the flour and a pinch of salt in a bowl and rub in the butter until you have a mixture resembling fine breadcrumbs.
2. Make a well in the centre and bind with enough water to make a soft dough. Knead the pastry twice then cover and refrigerate until needed.
3. Butter a deep, straight-sided baking tin then sprinkle a layer of sugar about 1 cm (½") thick over the bottom of the tin. Fill with the apples.
4. Cut the butter up into small pieces and place on top of the apples then sprinkle with the remaining sugar.
5. Cover the apples completely with the pastry and bake for about 30 minutes.
6. Slip a knife down the side of the tart and check that the apples are cooked and the sugar well caramelised.
7. Turn it out on a serving dish with the pastry underneath and the caramelised apples on top. Serve hot.

"The friendly cow, all red and white,
I love with all my heart:
She gives me cream with all her might,
To eat with apple-tart."

A Child's Garden of Verses, 'The Cow'
ROBERT LOUIS STEVENSON, 1850-1894

CREPES PARISIENNES

Serves 8-10

Another French favourite from Le Caveau's 'Club des Vins'.

Metric		lb/oz	U.S.A.
	For the pancakes:		
3	*Eggs*	3	3
125 g	*Flour, sifted*	4 oz	1 cup
300 ml	*Milk*	½ pt	1 cup
2 tbsp	*Oil for the batter*	2 tbsp	2 tbsp
	Oil for frying		
400 g	*Fruit salad, can of*	14 oz	14 oz
50 g	*Icing sugar, sifted*	2 oz	½ cup
	For the custard:		
3	*Egg yolks*	3	3
40 g	*Caster sugar*	1½ oz	3 tbsp
40 g	*Flour, sifted*	1½ oz	⅓ cup
150 ml	*Milk*	¼ pt	½ cup

1. Beat the eggs in a bowl, stir in the flour and a pinch of salt. Pour on the milk and oil and beat the batter well.
2. Leave to stand, preferably refrigerated for 1-2 hours.
3. Heat the oil in the pan and make 8-10 pancakes putting them in a clean folded tea towel as they are made.
4. To make the custard beat the egg yolks with the sugar until you have a creamy consistency. Stir in the flour and milk. Pour into a pan and bring slowly to the boil stirring all the time until the custard thickens.
5. Divide between the pancakes, about 2 tbsp in each.
6. Strain the fruit and divide between the pancakes. Roll neatly and place in an ovenproof dish.
7. Sprinkle with the icing sugar and put under a very hot grill until the sugar is melted and golden.

CHOCOLATE ALMOND CRUNCH

This delicious crunch from the City Arts Centre is thoroughly addictive! It stores well in plastic tubs, each layer separated by tin foil.

Metric		lb/oz	U.S.A.
350 g	*Digestive biscuits, crushed*	12 oz	¾ lb
125 g	*Margarine*	4 oz	½ cup
6 tbsp	*Golden syrup*	6 tbsp	½ cup
125 g	*Sultanas*	4 oz	⅔ cup
50 g	*Glacé cherries, chopped*	2 oz	¼ cup
125 g	*Blanched almonds, chopped*	4 oz	1 cup
50 g	*Cocoa powder*	2 oz	¼ cup
125 g	*Plain cooking chocolate*	4 oz	4 squares

1. Put the margarine, syrup, sultanas, cherries, almonds and cocoa powder into a pan and place over a gentle heat. Stir continuously for about five minutes when the syrup and margarine will be melted and the cocoa powder mixed in. Pour on to the biscuits and mix well.
2. Grease a 25×30 cm ($10'' \times 12''$) baking tray, fill with the mixture and smooth and flatten with a metal spoon.
3. Put the chocolate in a basin over a pan of hot water until melted. Pour evenly over the biscuit mixture.
4. Refrigerate to set and cut into small squares when cold.

ANN STREET

Find the time to visit this lovely and extremely unusual Georgian street, built by the artist Sir Henry Raeburn and taking its name from his wife, to whom it remains as a graceful and serene memorial.

The long gardens are green and decked with graceful trees, and amongst many unusual features worthy of note are the tall lamps worked into the iron work of the railings.

OATMEAL ROCKBUNS   *Makes about 15*

Clarinda's typically Scottish variation on a familiar tea-time treat is, of course, made with traditional porridge oats!

Metric		lb/oz	U.S.A.
250 g	*Self-raising flour*	8 oz	2 cups
250 g	*Porridge oats*	8 oz	2 cups
175 g	*Margarine*	6 oz	1 cup
175 g	*Caster sugar*	6 oz	¾ cup
175 g	*Mixed fruit*	6 oz	1 cup
1 tsp	*Mixed spice*	1 tsp	1 tsp
2	*Eggs, beaten*	2	2
1 tbsp	*Golden syrup*	1 tbsp	1 tbsp

1. Set the oven to 180°C, 350°F, Gas Mark 4.
2. Place the flour and porridge oats in a mixing bowl and rub in the margarine. Stir in the sugar, fruit and spice.
3. Make a well in the centre and add the eggs. Mix well.
4. Add the syrup and stir in to make a soft dough.
5. Place 15 rough heaps on to a greased baking tray and bake in the centre of the oven for about 25 minutes.

"A grain, which in England is generally given to horses, but in Scotland supports the people."
> Dictionary of the English Language: oatmeal
> DR SAMUEL JOHNSON, 1709-1784

NUTTY OATCAKES

A teatime treat using a mixture of fine and medium oatmeal from Scottish cook, Mrs. Betty Boyd.

Metric		lb/oz	U.S.A.
175 g	*Pinhead oatmeal*	6 oz	1½ cups
175 g	*Medium oatmeal*	6 oz	1½ cups
175 g	*Plain flour*	6 oz	1½ cups
½ tsp	*Salt*	½ tsp	½ tsp
½ tsp	*Sugar*	½ tsp	½ tsp
1 tsp	*Baking powder*	1 tsp	1 tsp
175 g	*Roast beef dripping or cooking fat*	6 oz	¾ cup

1. Set the oven to 180°C, 350°F, Gas Mark 4.
2. Mix the dry ingredients and rub in the fat. Add enough warm water to form a stiff dough.
3. Roll out the dough on a floured board until it is about ½ cm (¼") thick. Cut into round shapes.
4. Place on a greased baking tray and bake for 30 minutes until pale brown.

THE ROYAL BOTANIC GARDEN is well worth a visit. See also
page 69.

LEMON AND ALMOND SHORTBREAD

A rich version of a traditional delicacy from Le Jardin.

Metric		lb/oz	U.S.A.
50 g	Icing sugar, sifted	2 oz	½ cup
50 g	Caster sugar	2 oz	¼ cup
200 g	Butter	8 oz	1 cup
200 g	Plain flour	8 oz	2 cups
100 g	Cornflour	4 oz	¾ cup
50 g	Flaked almonds	2 oz	⅔ cup
2 tsp	Lemon peel	2 tsp	2 tsp

1. Set the oven to 170°C, 325°F, Gas Mark 3.
2. Place the icing sugar, caster sugar and butter together in a bowl and beat until creamy then add the flour and cornflour and mix well.
3. Add almost all the almonds and knead until smooth.
4. Place on a floured board and roll out into a large round 2 cm (¾") thick. Make smaller rounds or fingers if liked.
5. Sprinkle the remaining almonds and lemon peel on top. Press into the mixture by rolling gently with a rolling pin.
6. Decorate the edges by pinching with the finger and thumb.
7. Place in the centre of the oven and cook for ¾-1 hour until golden brown.

COUNTRY TASTE SHORTBREAD

Traditional Scottish shortbread guaranteed to melt in your mouth!

Metric		lb/oz	U.S.A.
125 g	*Butter*	4 oz	½ cup
60 g	*Caster sugar*	2 oz	½ cup
125 g	*Plain flour*	4 oz	1 cup
60 g	*Rice flour*	2 oz	½ cup

1. Set the oven to 160°C, 325°F, Gas Mark 3.
2. Cream the butter and sugar together until light and fluffy.
3. Mix the two flours together and gradually work into the butter mixture until it resembles shortcrust pastry.
4. Divide the dough into two pieces and place on a baking tray. Shape each into an oblong about 2 cm (¾") thick.
5. Prick all over with a fork and pinch the edges to decorate.
6. Bake for 45 minutes until golden brown.
7. Remove from the oven and sprinkle with a little additional caster sugar. Cut while still warm.

PEPPERMINT BAR

Chocolate and peppermint combine in this tried and trusted tray bake recipe, from Clarinda's Tea Room.

Metric		lb/oz	U.S.A.
225 g	Margarine	8 oz	1 cup
125 g	Caster sugar	4 oz	½ cup
150 g	Self-raising flour	5 oz	1¼ cups
150 g	Plain flour	5 oz	1¼ cups
175 g	Desiccated coconut	6 oz	1½ cups
1 tbsp	Cocoa powder, sieved	1 tbsp	1 tbsp
60 g	Chocolate	2 oz	2 squares
	For the peppermint cream:		
2	Egg whites	2	2
225 g	Icing sugar, sifted	8 oz	2 cups
1 tsp	Peppermint essence	1 tsp	1 tsp

1. Set the oven to 180°C, 350°F, Gas Mark 4.
2. Cream together the margarine and sugar until light and fluffy. Stir in the dry ingredients and mix well.
3. Press into a greased Swiss roll tin and bake for 20-30 minutes. Cool on a wire rack.
4. To make the peppermint cream, whisk the egg whites until stiff and firm then fold in the icing sugar, using enough to make the mixture firm. Stir in the essence.
5. When the base is cool, spread the peppermint mixture over. Melt the chocolate in a basin over a pan of hot water then carefully cover the peppermint cream.
6. Allow the chocolate to set, then cut into squares.

MARY KING'S CLOSE, the street beneath the High Street, is not to be found on today's street maps. So many of its inhabitants died of the Black Death, that in 1645 the entire Close, much of it already abandoned, was closed for fear of the plague spreading. Apart from being opened for inspection when the City Chambers were under construction, it has stood deserted for over 300 years!

Mary King's Close is said to be haunted both by plague victims and Mary King herself. It can still be reached through the cellars, but only by special arrangement with the Council. The Close ran down the steep rock face and was completely covered by the City Chambers which rise four stories on High Street and plummet twelve stories down on the north side.

GIANT LILIES IN THE ROYAL BOTANIC GARDEN

Resembling huge, floating tea trays, these horticultural giants are to be found in the hot houses of the Botanic Garden.

GIANT THISTLES, Scotland's national emblem flower, can also be found — spot them in Princes St. Gardens.

Choux Pastry

Metric		lb/oz	U.S.A.
50 g	Butter	2 oz	¼ cup
65 g	Plain flour	2½ oz	½ cup
2	Eggs	2	2

1. Set the oven to 200°C, 400°F, Gas Mark 6.
2. Heat the butter with 150 ml (¼ pt, ½ cup) water on a low heat until melted. Pour the sifted flour and a pinch of salt quickly into the butter and water. Remove from the heat and stir vigorously until smooth. Set aside to cool slightly.
3. Beat the eggs lightly and add them to the paste a little at a time. The paste should become a smooth and shiny ball.
4. Pipe on to a damp baking sheet. Bake for 10 minutes, then turn up to 220°C, 425°F, Gas Mark 7, for about 15 minutes until crisp and golden. Cool on a rack.

SAUCES

Tomato sauce

Metric		lb/oz	U.S.A.
1	Onion, chopped	1	1
1 tbsp	Oil	1 tbsp	1 tbsp
1 tsp	Basil or marjoram	1 tsp	1 tsp
1	Garlic clove, crushed	1	1
400 g	Tomatoes, can of	14 oz	14 oz
2 tsp	Tomato purée	2 tsp	2 tsp

1. Fry the onion in the oil with the herbs and garlic until transparent but not brown.
2. Sieve or liquidize the tomatoes.
3. Stir in the tomatoes and purée and simmer for 20 minutes.

Hollandaise sauce

Metric		lb/oz	U.S.A
4 tbsp	White wine vinegar	4 tbsp	5 tbsp
1 tsp	Lemon juice	1 tsp	1 tsp
1 tbsp	Onion, chopped	1 tbsp	1 tbsp
1	Bay leaf	1	1
1	Blade of mace	1	1
6	Peppercorns	6	6
3	Egg yolks	3	3
125 g	Softened butter	5 oz	⅔ cup
2 tbsp	Single cream	2 tbsp	3 tbsp

1. Boil the vinegar, lemon juice, onion, bay leaf, mace and peppercorns in a small pan until the liquid is reduced to about 1 tablespoon.
2. Beat the yolks in a bowl with a nut of·butter and a pinch of salt until light and fluffy. Strain liquid and add to yolks.
3. Stand the bowl on top of a pan of boiling water and add the rest of the butter in small pieces, beating continuously until thick and creamy. Stir in cream and season to taste.

Demi-glace sauce

To make a demi-glace sauce, put equal quantities of Espagnole sauce (below) and strong beef stock into a heavy pan (with a few mushrooms if available).

Simmer until the sauce is reduced by at least half. Remove, strain and re-heat. Remove from the heat and stir in a small glassful of dry sherry.

Espagnole sauce

Metric		lb/oz	U.S.A.
25 g	Ham or bacon (raw), chopped	1 tbsp	1 tbsp
25 g	Butter	1 oz	1 tbsp
1	Carrot, peeled and chopped	1	1
1	Onion	1	1
3 tbsp	Mushroom stalks, chopped	3 tbsp	⅓ cup
2 tbsp	Celery, chopped (optional)	2 tbsp	¼ cup
40 g	Flour	1½ oz	¼ cup
1	Beef stock cube	1	1
2 tbsp	Tomato paste	2 tbsp	¼ cup
250 g	Tomatoes, peeled and chopped	½ lb	1 cup
1 tsp	Thyme	1 tsp	1 tsp
1	Bay leaf	1	1

1. Cook the bacon in the butter for a few minutes.
2. Add the vegetables and sauté gently for 5-8 minutes.
3. Make a stock with the cube and 300 ml (½ pt, 1 cup) boiling water. Set aside.
4. Stir the flour into the vegetable mixture. Continue stirring until the flour browns well, then add the stock very gradually, stirring continuously.
5. When the sauce has thickened, stir in the tomato paste, tomatoes, thyme and bay leaf. Season lightly.
6. Simmer for 30 minutes, stirring occasionally and skimming off excess fat. Taste and correct the seasoning.
7. Strain the sauce into a basin and cover the surface with damp greaseproof or clingwrap to stop a skin forming.

The Edinburgh Festival

For three exhilarating weeks each summer, Edinburgh bursts forth into song, dance and drama, as actors, musicians, dancers and poets flock into the City to appear in one of the most celebrated occasions of the cultural world — The Edinburgh International Festival of Music and Drama.

How it all Began

The Festival made a fittingly dramatic entrance to the world in 1947 — a time of economic doldrums and general dreariness. The founders decided that a reminder of life's brighter side was needed, and set themselves to organizing a large-scale arts festival. Contrary to the thoughts of many pessimists, the first festival was a great success, delighting everybody concerned.

From Verdi's Requiem to street performers

Since then, the festival has grown considerably. Each year, a third of the programme illustrates the main theme, which has varied from celebrating the cultures of a particular country to commemorating a great composer.
One amusing incident occured in 1950 when Sir Thomas Beecham was persuaded to conduct Handel's 'Music for the Royal Fireworks'. He did so, but only after Lady Beecham had kitted him out with a steel helmet to protect him from falling Catherine wheels and flying sparks. (No doubt it complimented his 'tails'!)

The birth of the Fringe

The famous 'Fringe' originated in 1947 when eight unknown theatre groups arrived in Edinburgh to add their own flavour to the programme. Today 300 companies present the diverse programme that includes mime, melodrama and street theatre (performed anywhere and everywhere with handprops, masks and costume). Dull and predictable it certainly isn't! Strolling minstrels, actors and singers make names for themselves through the Fringe.

The festival and the people

The Festival cavalcade passing through Princes Street heralds the start of another exciting three weeks of festivities — the drama, music, and dance which is now a deeply rooted part of the Edinburgh calendar.

MEASURES & CONVERSIONS

Please read the notes on measures and conversions on page 4.
The table below will help our American readers.

English	**American**
Bicarbonate of soda	Baking soda
Caster sugar	Fine granulated sugar
Cornflour	Cornstarch
Desiccated coconut	Shredded coconut
Digestive biscuits	Graham crackers
Double cream	Heavy cream
Flaked almonds	Slivered almonds
Glacé cherries	Candied red cherries
Golden syrup	Light corn syrup
Icing sugar	Confectioners' sugar
Plain chocolate	Semi-sweet chocolate
Single cream	Light cream
Sultanas	Light raisins

A HAIR-RAISING TALE!

The story of Burke and Hare is a gory and nightmarish part of Edingburgh's past. Only hanged criminals could legally be used for anatomical research, and the illegal practice of body-snatching from graves was widespread and much feared. These two unsavoury characters decided to save themselves the trouble of digging by simply murdering their victims!
When Hare informed on his partner, thus saving his own skin (literally, as it turns out!). Burke underwent a grim sort of justice: he was hanged in the Lawnmarket and his body delivered to the University's Department of Anatomy for dissection. His skeleton can still be seen there!

Index

GREYFRIARS BOBBY

Greyfriars Bobby was a little Skye terrier who so won the hearts of the people of Edinburgh by his extraordinary devotion to his deceased master that a statue was erected to him at the top of Candlemakers' Row. When his master died Bobby kept guard over his grave until his own death some 14 years later. A great favourite with local children, he was liable to be destroyed when a new dog licensing law was introduced. Such was the strength of feeling that the Lord Provost stepped in to save Bobby by buying him a special collar.

RESTAURANTS & HOTELS

We would like to thank the following for their help and generosity in giving us the recipes listed below. Local telephone numbers are also provided.

MRS. BETTY BOYD, formerly of 'Country Taste'.

CALEDONIAN HOTEL, Princes Street   225 2433
POMPADOUR RESTAURANT
Executive chef: Alan Hill
    Wild Highland mussels, 19
    Cocktail Glendronach, 20
    Peach Highland cream, 52
Luncheon: 12.30-2.30 pm (7 days)
Dinner: 6-10 pm (7 days)

CITY ARTS CENTRE CAFE, 1 Market Street   225 2424
    Crunchy cream cheese salad, 50
    Green bean and mushroom salad, 50
    City Arts' special, 50
    Mandarin cream pie, 62
    Chocolate almond crunch, 64
Open: 8.30 am-4.30 pm (Mon-Sat). 8.30 am-5.30 pm (June-Sept)

CLARINDA'S TEA ROOM, 69 Canongate   557 1888
Proprietress/chef: Marion Thomson
    Oatmeal rockbuns, 66
    Peppermint bar, 69
Open: 8.30 am-4.45 pm (Mon-Sat). 10 am-4.45 pm (Sun)

COUSTEAUS' RESTAURANT, 109 Hanover Street   226 3355
Chef: Mr. Le Cornec
    Homard Hebridean, 27
    Bananes au rhum et café, 55
Dinner: 6-Midnight (Mon-Sat)

CRINGLETIE HOUSE HOTEL, Peebles   07213 233
Chef: Aileen Maguire
    Chinese vegetable soup, 15
    Avocado with cheese and fresh herbs, 18
    Lamb cutlets persille, 31
    Gypsy potatoes, 51
    Butterscotch velvet, 55
    Orange cheesecake, 61
Luncheon: 1-1.45 pm.Dinner: 7.30-8.30 pm (7 days)

DENZLER'S, 80 Queen Street   226 5467
Head chef: Frank Fusco
    Veau à la limone, 34
    Chicken Seville, 36
    Bananes à la Gruyère, 54
    Sabayon glacée au vin blanc, 54
Luncheon: 12-2 pm. Dinner: 6.30-10 pm (Mon-Sat)

ELLERSLY HOUSE HOTEL, Ellersly Road, Murrayfield   337 6888
Chef: G. Hogg
    Scotch broth, 14
    Soused herrings, 18
    Fillet Ellersly, 30
    Stoved howtowdie, 37
Luncheon: 12.30-2 pm. Dinner: 7-9 pm (7 days)

KING JAMES HOTEL, St. James Centre   556 0111
Chef: Ronnie Reglinski
  Partan bree, 12
  Blue Stuart fillet, 28
Luncheon: 12.30-2.30 pm. Dinner: 6.30-10.30 pm (7 days)

LE CAVEAU "CLUB DES VINS", 13b Dundas Street   556 5707
Proprietor: François Aliane
Chef: Jean-Marie Meny
  Le Caveau's onion tart, 16
  Timbale de rognons Dijonnaise, 33
  Crêpes surprises, 45
  Tarte tatin, 63
  Crêpes Parisiennes, 64
Luncheon: 12-2 pm. Dinner: 6-10 pm (Mon-Sat)

NIMMO'S, 101 Shandwick Place   229 6119
Proprietors: Mr and Mrs Nimmo
Chefs: Michael Brown and Paul Subido
  Pork Sandeman, 31
  Chicken tropicana, 37
  Virginia chicken and apple salad, 47
  Nimmo's pickled cucumber, 51
Luncheon: 12-2.30 pm (Mon-Fri)
Dinner: 6.30-10.30 pm (Sun-Fri)

POST HOUSE HOTEL, Costorphine Road   334 8221
Head chef: A. Mackay
  Avocado Marriane, 16
  Chicken Craigellachle, 38
Luncheon: 12.30-2 pm. Dinner: 7-10.30 pm (7 days)

ROXBURGHE HOTEL, 38 Charlotte Square   225 3921
Head chef: William Marshall
  Pickled lemon kippers, 19
  Cheesey veal Madeira, 35
Luncheon: 12-2 pm (Mon-Fri)
Dinner: 6-10 pm (Mon-Sat) 6-9.30 pm (Sun)

RUTLAND HOTEL, 3 Rutland Street   229 3402
LE JARDIN RESTAURANT
Chef Sneden
  Cock-a-leekie soup, 13
  Entrecôte steak Glen Isla, 30
  Haunch of venison Bonnie Prince Charlie, 38
  Edinburgh fog, 53
  Lemon and almond shortbread, 67
Luncheon: 12-2 pm. Dinner: 7-10 pm. (7 days)

THE LAIGH KITCHEN, 117a Hanover Street   225 1552
Proprietress/chef: Joan Spicer
  Pears in blue cheese, 17
Open: 9 am-2 pm (Mon & Sat). 9 am-5 pm(Tues-Fri)

L'AUBERGE RESTAURANT FRANCAIS, 56 St Mary's Street
Proprietor: Daniel Wencker   556 5888
Chef: Daniel Martelat
  Lapin rôti au miel, 44
Luncheon: 12.30-2 pm (7 days)
Dinner: 6.30-9.30 pm (7 days), 6.30-10.30 pm (Fri-Sat)

THE ROYAL SCOT HOTEL, 111 Glasgow Road   334 9191
Chef: J. Dobbie
  Canapé Caledonian, 20
  Cottage cheese and pineapple mousse, 21
Luncheon: 12.30-2.30 pm. Dinner: 7-10.30 pm
Closed Sundays

THE MILITARY TATTOO *(page 72/3)*

Parades of Scottish pipers and drummers, exotic displays from overseas, military groups in colourful regimental costumes, young soldiers and Scottish maidens energetically dancing the Highland Fling all merge to present the spectacular Tattoo for three thrilling weeks during Festival time.

It is interesting to note that the word 'tattoo' originally had more in common with alcohol than parades. A drum beat 'tap-to' was sounded nightly to warn soldiers to return to their quarters and publicans to stop serving them!

Set in the floodlit grounds of the castle esplanade and complimenting the grandeur of the event, the Tattoo also has the reputation of inspiring overwhelming feelings of unity when, at the end of each performance, its vast audience join hands to sing 'Auld Lang Syne'. Next time you hear it, remember Edinburgh and that warm Scottish farewell 'Haste ye back'.

'Should auld acquaintance be forgot
And never brought to mind,
Should auld acquaintance be forgot,
And auld lang syne.

For auld lang syne my dear,
For auld lang syne,
We'll tak a cup o' kindness yet,
For auld lang syne.'

Titles in print:
Bath, Cambridge, Stratford,
Oxford, the Cotswolds,
York and Harrogate, and Edinburgh

In preparation:
Brighton,
Cheltenham and Gloucester
Hampstead and Highgate